Security

vs.

Access

Balancing Safety and Productivity
in the Digital School

LeAnne K. Robinson
Abbie H. Brown
Tim D. Green

International Society for Technology in Education
EUGENE, OREGON · WASHINGTON, DC

Security vs. Access

Balancing Safety and Productivity in the Digital School

LeAnne K. Robinson, Abbie H. Brown, and Tim D. Green

© 2010 International Society for Technology in Education

Director of Book Publishing: *Courtney Burkholder*
Acquisitions Editor: *Jeff V. Bolkan*
Production Editors: *Lanier Brandau, Tina Wells*
Production Coordinator: *Rachel Williams*
Graphic Designer: *Signe Landin*
Copy Editor: *Kathy Hamman*
Proofreader: *Anna Drexler*
Cover Design, Book Design, and Production: *Signe Landin*

Library of Congress Cataloging-in-Publication Data

Robinson, LeAnne.
  Security vs. access : balancing safety and productivity in the digital school / LeAnne K. Robinson, Abbie H. Brown, Tim D. Green. — 1st ed.
      p. cm.
  Includes bibliographical references.
  ISBN 978-1-56484-264-0 (pbk.)
  1. Internet in education—Security measures—United States. 2. Computer security—Study and teaching—United States. 3. Information technology—Study and teaching—United States. I. Brown, Abbie. II. Green, Tim D. III. International Society for Technology in Education. IV. Title.
  LB1028.5.R545 2010
  371.33'44678—dc22

                                                                      2009053207

First Edition
ISBN: 978-1-56484-264-0

Printed in the United States of America

International Society for Technology in Education (ISTE)
Washington, DC, Office:
   1710 Rhode Island Ave. NW, Suite 900, Washington, DC 20036-3132
Eugene, Oregon, Office:
   180 West 8th Ave., Suite 300, Eugene, OR 97401-2916
Order Desk: 1.800.336.5191
Order Fax: 1.541.302.3778
Customer Service: orders@iste.org
Book Publishing: books@iste.org
Book Sales and Marketing: booksmarketing@iste.org
Web: www.iste.org

Photos: ©iStockphoto.com
Cover, chapters 2 & 5, Winterling; Chapter 1, Kirill Bodrov; Chapter 3, DNY59; Chapter 4, Sndr; Chapter 6, Ozgur Onal; Chapter 7, Zentilia; Chapter 8, Kim Harris.

ISTE® is a registered trademark of the International Society for Technology in Education.

About ISTE

The International Society for Technology in Education (ISTE) is the trusted source for professional development, knowledge generation, advocacy, and leadership for innovation. ISTE is the premier membership association for educators and education leaders engaged in improving teaching and learning by advancing the effective use of technology in PK–12 and teacher education.

Home of the National Educational Technology Standards (NETS) and ISTE's annual conference and exposition (formerly known as NECC), ISTE represents more than 100,000 professionals worldwide. We support our members with information, networking opportunities, and guidance as they face the challenge of transforming education. To find out more about these and other ISTE initiatives, visit our website at **www.iste.org**.

As part of our mission, ISTE Book Publishing works with experienced educators to develop and produce practical resources for classroom teachers, teacher educators, and technology leaders. Every manuscript we select for publication is carefully peer-reviewed and professionally edited. We value your feedback on this book and other ISTE products. E-mail us at **books@iste.org**.

About the Authors

LeAnne K. Robinson (Leanne.robinson@wwu.edu), a former classroom and special education teacher, has authored a number of books and journal articles on educational technology. Robinson is an associate professor in the Department of Special Education and Program in Instructional Technology at Woodring College of Education, Western Washington University. She received her PhD in education from Washington State University.

Abbie H. Brown (brownab@ecu.edu) is an associate professor specializing in instructional design and technology at East Carolina University in the College of Education's Department of Mathematics, Science, and Instructional Technology Education. An award-winning teacher, he helps educators in K–12, college, government, and corporate settings understand and apply the instructional design process. Dr. Brown is the editor-in-chief of the journal *TechTrends*. You are invited to visit www.ahbrown.com and view a short movie about his Second Life office hours.

Tim D. Green (timdgreen@gmail.com), an author of ed tech books and a former elementary and middle school teacher, is currently an associate professor at California State University, Fullerton. Green conducts research on online teaching and learning, 1 to 1 computing, and integrating technology into teaching and learning processes. Dr. Green was formerly the director of distance education for California State University, Fullerton. You are welcome to visit www.drtimgreen.com.

Acknowledgments

We are indebted to everyone at ISTE for their help and support in the creation of this book. A huge *thank you!* to Lanier Brandau, Megan Dolman, Lynda Gansel, and Tina Wells for their efforts on the book's behalf.

We are especially grateful for Jeff Bolkan's guidance in suggesting we expand our article "The Threat of Security: Hindering Technology Integration in the Classroom" that appeared in *Learning & Leading with Technology* to book form, and for serving as the text's editor.

Dedication

For my family and friends—LR

For Paul—AB

For J, B, and H. Thanks for your continual support!—TG

Contents

Contents

Introduction

We, the authors, teach a variety of instructional technology courses to inservice teachers. Our assignments usually include real-life applications of web and Internet projects. Earlier in our careers, teachers had unlimited access to the Internet, and challenges with completing assignments generally involved a lack of access to quality technology. Several years ago, the difficulty with completing assignments made a marked shift from inadequate hardware and software to a lack of access to the web and Internet.

When we talked with teachers and school media specialists and raised the issue of access with university colleagues around the country, a common theme emerged—the more fearful a district was about threats to security, the more tightly controlled access to the Internet (and computing hardware) became. We began keeping track of stories shared by school professionals about the many measures schools and school districts were taking to ensure that computing networks were safe from hackers and virus attacks, that students were protected from inappropriate content and activities, and that teachers and staff were using time and resources appropriately. These stories ranged from measures that worked well in schools to stories that seemed unbelievable because the security measures made computing tools almost impossible for teachers and students to use. Over time we noticed that teachers who had been challenged and frustrated with restrictions related to district security measures seemed less willing to use technology in their classrooms.

This book is an attempt to initiate constructive dialogue and critical conversations around security measures and the effects these measures have on teachers' abilities and willingness to integrate technology into teaching and learning. Our goal is to encourage all stakeholders to make a united effort to face these problems together to generate solutions that work for all school users of technology—teachers, students, administrators, and information technology (IT) specialists.

Chapters 2–8 start with real-life anecdotes based on personal experiences of teachers or taken from media sources. These anecdotes are followed with a brief description of the security threat and common misperceptions related to that threat. We then describe the realities of the problem, common responses, and recommendations for dealing with the threat. Although we do try to provide constructive solutions, this is not intended to be a guidebook. While we don't have all the solutions, we believe the only way to arrive at those solutions is to begin discussing the problems.

Because most of our stories come to us from teachers in the classroom and our career efforts focus on empowering teachers with technology, we often describe problems from the teachers' perspective. We recognize that everyone involved in keeping schools secure has the best interest of students, teachers, and school districts at heart. Our goal is not to place blame on any one group for the problems that exist; instead, we aim to provide information that will help teachers, administrators, parents, and IT professionals engage in worthwhile conversations to build consensus and help create safe, secure, and effective learning environments.

Threats to security are real. Access limitations are real. However, we believe the threats can be managed and minimized when the realities of the threats are clearly described and understood. We recognize that this is not necessarily an easy task, as each stakeholder has different perspectives, experiences, and understandings. If we keep our focus on students and learning, we may be able to develop realistic solutions and compromises that will move us forward. We believe in the power of technology. Together, with common beliefs and concentrated efforts and actions, we can build and maintain the best possible learning environments for our students—now and in the future.

Chapter 1

The Threat of Security and Its Effect on Access

A few years ago, a dedicated high school science teacher, "Tom," shared a story regarding his allegedly inappropriate use of the Internet:

> I spent last Saturday in my classroom, getting ready for back to school. Before I left, I ordered half a dozen bulbs from an online flower company. Don, the personnel director, sent me an e-mail and stopped by my classroom to inform me that I was now being monitored for inappropriate uses of the Internet. He said that repeated violations would be noted in my personnel file.

Tom also shared that new computers purchased for his classroom were equipped with inoperable CD-RW drives. When he inquired as to why he could not burn a CD of a PowerPoint presentation, he was told, "The drives will not be made available for open use.

Teachers may violate copyright laws if they are allowed to freely burn CDs." Tom has decided to avoid the use of computing technology in his classroom; he no longer cares to deal with the conflicts and increased permissions needed to use the available technological resources:

> I am a good teacher. Sure, technology may be beneficial, but it is much easier to continue doing what I know works than to attempt to use technology that is riddled with roadblocks.

Unfortunately, this teacher's story is similar to the experiences of many others. When we shared these two incidents with several colleagues, it turned out that they, too, had been collecting stories. Since first hearing stories such as these, we have been gathering examples of how perceived "threats of security" are hampering the integration of technology in teaching and learning (Robinson, Brown, & Green, 2004, 2007). After examining many similar reports from PK–12 schools and institutions of higher education, we asked ourselves the question: Could concerns over security be generating a fear that is now hindering the integration of technology? Our goals in this book are twofold: to help educators examine and analyze the challenges of increased security demands related to technology and to suggest ways that security measures might enhance rather than detract from the use of technology for learning.

We want to state clearly that we believe security is important. The safety of our children is of paramount concern, and our huge financial investment in networks, hardware, software, and infrastructure should be protected. Most of us have experienced the grinding halt to productivity that occurs when a system is attacked by a virus. We know that the reports of young people hurt by cybercrime are real. Other threats to our computer systems and students are real. Some teachers may not use technology responsibly. However, we cannot protect students by stifling all technology-based communication, and if protecting technology investments actually decreases or impedes the use of technology, then our goal of improving student learning through the integration of technology in PK–12 curriculums becomes more difficult if not impossible.

Education literature is replete with descriptions of barriers to the integration of technology (Robinson, 2003). These barriers include a lack of appropriate hardware and software, a lack of training, insufficient administrative support, and collegial jealousy. A lack of security measures, as far as we have found, has not been identified as a barrier. Studies indicate that teachers who use technology in their classrooms tend to develop and implement more constructivist, student-centered learning activities (Becker, 2000). Using technology in the classroom does not replace teachers, nor does its use mean that students are expected to discover every concept they learn by themselves. Rather, technology can serve as an effective tool that helps students become more involved in and excited by learning. Using computers in classrooms so that students may access the Internet can open up the world to students in visual and interactive ways that listening to a lecture and taking notes (and other teacher-centered forms of instruction) cannot accomplish. Therefore, we believe that the presence of technology in PK–12 classrooms is a contributing factor toward the development of authentic, engaging learning environments.

The full integration of technology into teaching and learning has been a relatively slow process, especially in PK–12 schools (Kalkowski, 2001). Access to technology has been identified as a contributing barrier to technology integration, yet increased access to technology was identified as a necessary goal by the CEO Forum (1999) during earlier integration efforts. Lack of access was listed as a primary barrier to technology integration (Ertmer, Addison, Lane, Ross, & Woods, 1999), and the International Society for Technology in Education (ISTE, 2000, 2008) explicitly states that access to technology is one of the necessary conditions for full integration. Schools across the nation have spent billions of dollars on computing technologies. The concerted effort to provide access to computing technology has resulted in wired schools, where students and educators have educational technology available in a large percentage of teaching and learning situations.

With the ongoing development of computing infrastructure and increased access to the world of networked computers, school districts have been encouraged to examine issues of security. Early security measures in PK–12 schools focused on cybersecurity for students, including limiting access to inappropriate websites. Schools purchased programs that blocked student access to particular sites on the Internet. In attempts to protect students, limit liability, and receive federal funding, district technology committees implemented Internet Use Policies (now commonly referred to as Acceptable Use Policies or AUPs), which had to be signed by parents. Students had to comply with and teachers were expected to enforce the policies. Students who violated their schools' AUPs lost Internet privileges. In addition, school districts purchased antivirus software, made efforts to increase firewall security, and started backing up data. A third line of security included the development of protocols for accessing network information.

In recent years, educators have become increasingly aware of copyright law. School district staff and faculty are expected to monitor potential copyright infringement associated with digital information accessed through the web, and they must ensure that software use adheres to licensing policies and restrictions. Furthermore, teachers who have traditionally made use of copyrighted materials within the relative safety of their own classrooms find themselves having to deal with larger issues of copyright infringement as they display classroom content on the Internet. Most teachers do not worry about using a picture of Snoopy or Scooby-Doo to brighten a classroom bulletin board, but those same teachers may be genuinely frightened at the prospect of prosecution for using that same picture on a classroom-related web page.

It has been established that the mere presence of computing technology does not promote access (Cuban, Kirkpatrick, & Peck, 2001). Although technologies may be present, many students and educators in PK–12 and in higher education are increasingly reporting problems with using technologies due to increased security measures. Employee-monitoring software typically used in business settings is now being used by administrators to monitor faculty use of the Internet and e-mail. Additionally, faculty members, like their students, are increasingly expected to read and follow strict AUPs. Although most security measures appear to be well grounded, there is increasing evidence that many policies imposed by administrators as good-faith efforts to protect students and personnel from danger are actually decreasing the availability and utility of integrating technology into teaching and learning. The more information we gather, the clearer it becomes that fear regarding computing technology security is having a negative impact on students and educators.

We are concerned that many of the current and most common security measures are more punitive than supportive and that they will cause teachers to avoid integrating technology into their classrooms for fear of negative repercussions. In the worst-case scenario, teachers would make no attempt to experiment with or creatively apply innovative technologies to their teaching practices for fear of administrative reprimands. Those of us who believe in the power of computing tools as a positive force in the classroom must find ways to create environments where the potential dangers of the tools are minimized without minimizing teachers' opportunities for professional growth.

Examining Eight Security Threats

In the following chapters we examine eight security threats that directly affect educators and students:

1. Inappropriate content

2. Predators, or ensnarement

3. Misuse of mobile communication devices

4. Cyberbullying

5. Network security

6. Inappropriate network use

7. Copyright infringement

8. Data and identity theft

These threats are often misunderstood because of sensational reports in the media. As education professionals, our goal is to see beyond the sensationalism and deal with the realities of the situation. To that end, in their respective chapters we attempt to describe each security threat as it is generally perceived and then present the realities of the situation. We describe common solutions for each problem and recommend approaches that are professionally responsible.

We want every educator to see the truth of the situation. In some cases, the popular media have created a climate of fear where none should exist. Unfortunately, some real dangers do exist, but effective protections should not come at higher costs than the dangers warrant. In many cases, the dangers are real, but some people are addressing them incorrectly. In the chapters that follow, we discuss the facts regarding our greatest computer security concerns and recommend measures to deal effectively with those concerns.

Chapter 2

Inappropriate Content

A parent helping her daughter with a report for school looked up "horse lovers" on the web and was presented with a website completely inappropriate for the activity, "... horse lovers of a COMPLETELY different kind ..." (Workman, 2007).

❧

Teenagers who might never have been exposed to gang life are able to view gang violence and gang lifestyles through social networking sites. Flashing gang signs because they thought it was funny, teenagers are threatened by actual gang members who are not at all amused (Menillo, 2009).

❧

Three Hong Kong teenagers were arrested for possessing explosives of the type used in the 2005 London suicide attacks.

Police suspect the 13- and 14-year-olds learned how to make the bombs online ("HK Teens," *Agence France-Presse*, 2009).

༄

The Threat

This generation of students is the first to grow up with the Internet as part of everyday life. More than 21 million young people in the U.S., 87%, use the Internet. Almost two-thirds of them use the Internet at school (Hitlin & Rainie, 2005), and this number is rising. Teens report that although they do go online at school, school is not their only point of access; most (99%) use the Internet in multiple locations, such as home, another person's home, the library, or a community center (Hitlin & Rainie, 2005). More than half of students polled stated that the Internet is the most useful tool for help with homework (Livingstone & Bober, 2005).

As useful as it undeniably is, the web is also riddled with inappropriate and undesirable content. This includes sites with dangerous or illegal guides (such as bomb-making "cookbooks"), pornography, gruesome and violent pictures and sites, racist/hateful content, and advertising. Unfortunately, even best efforts to avoid inappropriate content do not prevent young people and adults from viewing unwanted content. In a UK study, it was found that 57% of youth ages 9–19 had viewed pornography on the Internet, and 22% accidentally ended up on sites with violent pictures (Livingstone & Bober, 2005). Access in the UK is similar to that in the United States, and all children likely follow these same patterns. No matter what your age, if you use the Internet, it is likely that you will come across some inappropriate content. The desire and need to protect our schools' students from potentially harmful or damaging sites has been present since the introduction of the Internet in the schools.

Common Misperceptions of the Threat

The major misperception regarding the viewing of inappropriate content is that content on the web can be completely controlled. As you'll see, the majority of measures are not 100% effective. A concern among people who work with young children is that they will be exposed to highly inappropriate content when they browse the web. The very young may inadvertently type in an incorrect web address or follow an innocuous link and find themselves presented with pornography, racist/hate sites, or sites that promote terrorism. The misperception is that this can be controlled. When individuals fail to realize this, major fears arise. For example, some administrators have fears that any inappropriate use of the Internet will jeopardize their school's funding. Teachers also fear that their association with an inappropriate site, even when accidentally opened, may be cause for a reprimand. Neither is usually the case.

Additional concerns surround intentional viewing of inappropriate sites by students, particularly adolescents. The misperception is that the majority of young people, when left to their own devices, will discover and dwell upon inappropriate content on the web.

There is a great deal of discussion about software that filters or blocks inappropriate content. Many individuals who may not fully understand how these software programs work have the misperception that the use of filters and blocks will fully protect students and schools.

The Realities of the Inappropriate Content Threat

Teachers have a variety of concerns in the classroom. The first mission of any teacher is student learning; teachers want to do everything they possibly can to make sure that students leave their classrooms with the skills and knowledge that they need to succeed at the next grade level and in the future. To this end, teachers provide all kinds of opportunities for learning and engagement, which can include (and, we would argue, should include) using the Internet. Although students' learning is the top priority, teachers are also concerned for students' safety. And, like every working person, most teachers are concerned about succeeding in and keeping their jobs. If teachers perceive that using a particular teaching tool, the Internet, potentially puts a district's funding at risk, and if teachers are worried about getting in trouble with parents and/or district administrators for potential breaches, using technology may not seem worthwhile, even if they know that students would benefit educationally. Losing funding or a job due to failure to monitor all students' computer use creates fear of Internet use.

Although the ultimate aim of Internet censorship is the well-being and safety of students, there are also concerns regarding district safety. Administrators strive to keep students safe, and they have the additional responsibility of protecting district finances. This includes making sure that laws and regulations are followed and district funds are used for students and operations, not for litigation. The Children's Internet Protection Act (CIPA) of 2000 made it a requirement that schools adopt policies to protect students from inappropriate content on the Internet if they wanted to receive federal E-rate funding, a program that makes telecommunication and digital technology more affordable for schools and libraries that meet certain criteria (CIPA, 2001). Safeguards include such things as an Internet safety policy and measures that block or filter Internet access to pictures that (a) are obscene, (b) are child pornography, or (c) are harmful to minors.

Teachers have often shared with us that it is easier not to use the Internet than it is to attempt to have students do research or projects knowing that there will be sites that are inadvertently blocked. Although many districts have procedures in place that allow a teacher (or a student) to write a letter requesting the release of a blocked site, such measures do not allow for "just in time" instruction, which often occurs in daily instruction. Additional concerns emerge with the cumbersome aspects of the restrictions caused by some filters.

At the time that this book was written, the Senate Bill "Protecting Children in the 21st Century Act" was pending approval (S. 49—110th Congress, 2007). This act would require direct supervision of students who access a commercial social networking website or chat room and would require education about Internet safety. Failure to enforce the policy would jeopardize federal E-rate funds. Even if this bill fails to pass, others are sure to follow as long as there are fears about content. Such bills create high-stakes scenarios for administrators who are ultimately responsible for the district's financial bottom line. In addition to the fear of loss of funding due to legal restrictions, school districts are concerned about lawsuits from parents of students who are exposed to inappropriate content. A further discussion on teachers' use of the Internet can be found in Chapter 6, Inappropriate Uses of the Network.

Common Responses

In an effort to solve the problem of inappropriate content, schools (and parents) have tried multiple ways to keep inappropriate content on the Internet from being accidentally or intentionally accessed by youth. The solutions described in this section include attempts at limiting access digitally, deterring intentional access through policy, and preventing exposure through direct supervision.

Filtering and Blocking Software

Installing filtering and/or blocking software are two common digital solutions selected by many school districts trying to protect students from accessing inappropriate sites on the Internet. There are important distinctions between the two kinds of software. Blocking software creates a list of sites that are blocked from view. Blocking software requires constant updating, using various methods, depending upon the software company. Some companies periodically update their lists, and some allow their users to add custom sites to the list. The problem is that the number of websites grows almost exponentially every day, making it very likely that inappropriate content may be accessed, even with the most diligent attempts to keep the list of blocked sites up to date.

Filtering software takes a slightly different approach, generally with two techniques to prevent access to content. The first type of filtering software uses a list of keywords. These words can be selected individually or within the context of other words. The largest complaint about filtering software is that many appropriate sites are accidentally blocked along with the inappropriate sites because they share particular words. For example, the word "breast" will block all sites that contain information on breast cancer (and even recipes that include chicken breasts in the ingredients). A second type of filtering software attempts to limit access to certain types of sites, like drug and alcohol sites or sites with sexual content. This type of filtering works in much the same way as keyword filtering, only it uses banks of keywords. Some software applications allow users to select which types of sites and word chains engage the filter, and others do not.

How well does filtering and blocking software work? In their 2006 public policy report on the effectiveness of blocking and filtering software, Heins and Feldman found that the "best" blocking software blocked 95% of sites in the pornography and erotica category; 75% in the bomb-making and terrorism category; and 65% in the racist, hate, white supremacist, and Nazi categories. The same report found that sites in the following categories were blocked less effectively: only 60% in art and photography were blocked; 40% in sex education; 30% in atheism and anti-church; 20% in gay rights and gay politics; and 15% in drug education (pp. 47–48). These statistics indicate that even with the best filtering and blocking software, avoiding certain types of content on the Internet cannot be guaranteed.

A further variable in the application of filtering and blocking software is deciding where this software is installed. Schools have two ways to attempt to control access digitally, either through installing software on individual workstations (clients' computers) or by using a proxy server. A proxy server is a remote computer that all individual workstations are routed through. Most school districts install filter or blocking software on the district's proxy server instead of on every computer.

Acceptable Use Policies and Contracts

In addition to filtering or blocking software, almost every school district has developed an acceptable use policy (AUP). These are the district's written rules and responsibilities for computer use that also outline consequences for failure to follow the rules. AUPs usually identify when and how students can use district-owned computers and Internet connections, the nature of the content that can be viewed or downloaded, and descriptions of unacceptable content that users may not access. Generally, all students and their parents are expected to sign the agreement before students are allowed to access the Internet at school. Some school districts also create AUPs for teachers and other school employees. In broad terms, most AUPs state that digital technologies of any kind on school property may be used only for sanctioned schoolwork and activities. Before acceptable use policies are updated, districts need to review their state guidelines.

It is worth noting that parents often create policies for home computer use. In a study by Alexandra Macgill (2007), parents report regulating both the media content viewed and the amount of time spent viewing media by their children. Nearly two-thirds have rules about the Internet sites that their teenagers are allowed to visit. The vast majority of students are accustomed to abiding by policies and agreements.

Direct Supervision

Simply put, direct supervision is when an adult monitors by observation what a student is accessing on the Internet. Some schools have attempted to implement a gradual release of responsibility by trying to supervise elementary students directly and providing more freedom and unsupervised time to high school students.

Another approach similar to direct supervision is the monitoring of a user's "history" folder (a record kept by the browser software of each site visited) or the installation of software that tracks history and maintains a list of sites visited and keys this to a user ID or specific computer. Lists can be generated through such automated reporting systems that show visited sites and trends of Internet use.

Recommendations

Protecting students from inappropriate content is not really up for debate; we all want students to be safe. We can do this by balancing potential risks with potentially powerful learning experiences. Ultimately, Internet literacy is crucial. Students often access the Internet outside of school hours when they are unsupervised and use computers without filters. This is not going to change. Especially with the upsurge of available Internet-enabled mobile technologies, young people will continue to use the Internet without adult supervision. We need to teach students how to be responsible consumers of the Internet and how to make good choices about what they view. This starts at home and is reinforced at school.

Professional responsibility must be placed back into the hands of the teachers. Teachers are responsible for what happens in their classrooms, but they should not be in constant fear of Internet infractions. How can this be accomplished? First, teachers can be reminded to start each school year by giving students explicit instructions regarding safe use of the Internet. They can teach students about responsible usage, including what is inappropriate, such as hate sites, violent sites, and adult sites. Students of all ages are capable of learning procedures for how to handle situations when inappropriate content is accidentally encountered at school and at home. Students must develop advanced decision-making skills about how to navigate the Internet. This includes more than being told what is "right" or "wrong" or "acceptable" or "unacceptable." Students can be taught to develop critical thinking skills about the quality and worthiness of sites. Teachers can model and discuss with students ethical and moral behavior when making personal choices online.

Teachers should be allowed to integrate Internet use with lessons when reasonable safeguards are in place. What are these safeguards? In addition to instructing students on responsible use and enforcing reasonable AUPs, teachers should monitor students while they are online and, if possible, routinely check the history files at the end of the day.

Exposure to inappropriate content will happen to both students and teachers, even with filters and blocking software. Just as in the anecdotes described at the beginning of the this chapter, a parent (or teacher) may accidentally stumble onto a pornographic site (horse lover), or students may intentionally seek out inappropriate content (bomb building). Statistics tell us that digital solutions are never 100% effective. However, relying solely on digital solutions that limit access is frustrating for students and teachers alike. There is much that we can do to proactively deal with inappropriate content. Students need to be taught how to avoid accessing undesirable content, and schools should have procedures in place for dealing with both accidental and intentional exposure. Teachers need to be given freedom to exercise professional judgment, and everyone must be aware that problems will arise. How we deal with these problems will ultimately teach and prepare our students to be responsible users of the Internet.

Chapter 3

Predators, or Ensnaring Young People

The poster is a picture of an older man in front of a computer keyboard; the headline reads, "Meet 10-Year-Old Becky's 12-Year-Old Internet Friend" (National Center for Missing and Exploited Children, 2008).

❧

The Dateline NBC television series *To Catch A Predator* exposes adults attempting to engage in sexual activity with young people.

❧

News stories regularly illustrate and warn of the dangers of Internet predators:

"Keeping Internet Predators at Bay." *USA Today* (Baig, 2003).

"MySpace, Facebook Attract Online Predators: Experts say be careful what you post online—somebody is always watching." MSNBC (Williams, 2006).

"States Fault MySpace on Predator Issues." *New York Times* (Stone, 2007).

The Threat

The people children encounter online are not always who they say they are, and their intentions can be malicious. There are adults who use Internet communications to engage in sexual activity with minors. A recent national survey indicates that nearly half of all parents of Grades K–8 students are concerned that predators could target their children while at school ("National Survey," *Business Wire*, 2008). This perceived threat has caused parents and school officials to become apprehensive about allowing students access to networked computers for fear of exposing them to physical danger from predators.

Predators are people who attempt to engage young people in sexual activity. According to the U.S. Federal Bureau of Investigation (FBI), networked computer communication has become one of the most prevalent techniques used by pedophiles to lure children into illicit sexual relationships and to share illegal images of minors. The Internet has dramatically increased sexual predators' abilities to contact potential victims and has increased their access to a community of people who share this preference (FBI, Innocent Images National Initiative, n.d.*a*). The FBI reports that child pornography and child sexual exploitation cases accounted for 39% of its Cyber Division investigations in 2007. Between 1996 and 2007, the number of opened child pornography or sexual exploitation cases rose from 113 to 2,443, an increase of 2,162%.

Common Misperceptions of the Threat

The popular perception of predatory behavior is that of an adult male using chat rooms or messaging to pose as a young person in order to lure very young children into places where they can be kidnapped and assaulted. The predator is generally imagined as a brutal and terrifying figure; the victim is generally imagined as a very young and naïve child.

Parents, teachers, and administrators are often concerned that young children will be lured by predators into giving out personal information that leads to their being harmed through abduction and assault. Furthermore, there is a concern that predators can gain this type of information from social networking sites, such as Facebook or MySpace.

The assumption is that the predator finds information online or fools the child through online communication into providing enough personal information to locate and kidnap the child. The predator may lurk at the child's school or home or trick the child into a meeting at some other location where the child is abducted and assaulted. However, this is not really what happens in most cases.

The Realities of the Sexual Predator Threat

The news media tend to portray Internet predators as men who target very young, naïve children in order to kidnap and brutalize them. However, the reality, according to researchers who study this problem, is that most victims are teenagers between the ages of 13 and 17 (Wolak, Finkelhor, Mitchell, & Ybarra, 2008). Although there is little research about online predators themselves, the available evidence suggests that they fall within a narrow range of the sex offender population that excludes violent or sadistic behaviors (Wolak et al., 2008).

In reality, most predation and ensnarement crimes involve adolescents. Very few involve young children. The crimes do not typically involve stalking, abduction, or violence. Typically, teenagers are approached online by adults attempting to engage in sexual activity, and a percentage of teens do interact with these predators. Some victims meet with predators after developing a level of trust in them via online communication (Finkelhor, 2008; Wolak et al., 2008).

The predator typically plays into a young person's need to connect with people, his or her search for information about sex, or possibly his or her search for romance. According to David Finkelhor (2008), director of the Crimes Against Children Research Center at the University of New Hampshire, the teenagers know or find out quickly that they are talking to an adult interested in sex, but they continue the conversation. Finkelhor also points out that most young people do not respond to predators' solicitations and are not particularly concerned by them: "… they regard them as litter on their information superhighway and just kind of blow them off."

Adolescents Accessible to Predators

Reports about Internet predators tend to suggest that online communication between adults who initiate sex crimes and youths is a new development in child sexual abuse, but this is not true. Although online communication is a new medium, nonforcible sex crimes against youth are not new or uncommon. All states have criminal laws against sexual activity with young people under a certain age. The age of consent varies by state and ranges between ages 14 and 18. Most states exempt peer relationships from criminal activity by requiring a significant difference in age between the people involved (Wolak et al., 2008). Crimes of this nature are commonly referred to as statutory rape.

A study conducted in 2005 by researchers at the Crimes Against Children Research Center at the University of New Hampshire (Wolak, Mitchell, & Finkelhor, 2006) indicates that as many as one in seven young people receive unwanted sexual solicitations while online. Of the young Internet users who participated in the study, 4% responded that they had received requests for nude or sexually explicit photographs of themselves; 9% of the young people who said they had received solicitations also responded that they were distressed by the incidents. However, Finkelhor (2008) points out that many of these solicitations are coming from other young people or people who are acting strange online but are not actually attempting to engage in sex. Finkelhor suggests that in actuality the number is probably more like one in 20 young people receiving an "aggressive sexual solicitation."

The most common threat online is discussion of sexual activity by people who never intend to make the event real. Adolescents and adults tend to experiment with different personae while online.

It is a way to explore behaviors that they may never engage in offline. Although many people working through these explorations do not intend to cause harm to others, they also do not take others' feelings into consideration. Even if a communication is not intended to become a real sexual encounter, unless everyone involved in the conversation is taking part with an understanding that this is, for at least one participant, an experiment in behaving differently, the person unaware of the other's intentions is at risk. Although presentations about predators seducing and abducting children through the Internet tend to be overblown, a great many adolescents do indeed receive sexual solicitations from individuals they meet online. Regardless of whether this carries over to an offline situation, the experience of being tricked, propositioned, ensnared, or used as an object by another person can be traumatic and must be considered a serious threat.

Journalist Andy Carvin (2008) sums up the realities of online sexual predation brought to light by the study published in *American Psychologist* (Wolak et al., 2008) particularly well in the following list:

- Internet offenders pretended to be teenagers in only 5% of the crimes studied by researchers.

- Nearly 75% of victims who met offenders face-to-face did so more than once.

- Online sex offenders are seldom violent, and cases involving stalking or abduction are very rare.

Youth who engaged in four or more risky online behaviors were much more likely to report receiving online sexual solicitations. The online risky behaviors included: (1) maintaining buddy lists that included strangers, (2) discussing sex online with people they did not know in person, (3) being rude online, or (4) being nasty online.

Although there has been a documented increase in crimes related to possession of child pornography, at this time there is no research-based evidence that suggests the Internet has caused an increase in sexual offense crimes (Wolak et al., 2008). Furthermore, the research indicates that use of social networking sites, such as Facebook, does not in itself increase a risk of victimization, nor does posting personal information online seem to be in and of itself a risky behavior (Wolak et al., 2008).

Sexual predators usually attempt to become friends with the victim first. Chat rooms where visitors address difficult experiences (loss and mourning, for example) make particularly good target areas for predators. The predator typically attempts to communicate with a child by presenting himself (or herself) as another young person and gains trust by offering sympathy and advice. According to FBI agent Peter Brust, predators often keep organized lists of potential victims, cataloging their interests and online activity schedules (Finkelhor, 2008). Although aggressive sexual solicitation and predation is not as common as suggested by the media, it does happen, and everyone must take actions to protect against it.

Young People Particularly Vulnerable to Predators

According to the report published in *American Psychologist* (Wolak et al., 2008), most young people who engage in online interactions with people they do not know are not at risk for sexual victimization. However, young people who engage in certain types of online communications or behaviors are at greater risk and are likely to receive aggressive sexual solicitations.

Risky behaviors include the following:

- Sending personal information (name, telephone number, pictures) to people unknown to them (Note that deliberately sending information to one person is different from publicly posting this information.)

- Talking online to unknown people about sex

- Visiting chat rooms and other areas designed for adolescents

Young people with histories of sexual or physical abuse and other troubled youth may be particularly vulnerable. Girls and boys who are gay or are questioning their sexual orientation are more vulnerable (Wolak et al., 2008).

Common Responses

Common responses to the threat of sexual predators are for adults to warn children not to talk to strangers and for the child to tell a trusted adult if he or she has been approached by a stranger or is the victim of abusive behavior. Filtering software is often put in place as a preventive measure as well. Many schools and school districts block social networking sites, such as Facebook and MySpace, as well as blogs, gaming sites, and instant messaging.

Recommendations

Although it is important to keep in mind that the predator threat is less than popular forms of media suggest, the threat itself is real, and parents, teachers, and administrators must take action to combat the problem.

In dealing with the threat of predators and ensnarement, open communication between young people and the adults responsible for their welfare is essential. Children and adolescents need to know it is okay to talk with responsible adults about this issue. Parents and guardians need to take a proactive approach to monitoring young people's online activity.

Parents, teachers, and administrators often do not know how to use online communication and social networking tools as adeptly as young people do. However, this should not be an excuse to give young people total decision-making responsibility regarding the use of these tools. Most young people are not mature enough to understand the impact of their online activities. Parents and professional educators must take responsibility for learning about the tools and monitoring their uses.

The most common threat of sexual predation is not a pedophile attempting to attract a naïve young child by pretending to be another child; instead, it is more likely to be an adult attempting to ensnare a vulnerable teenager into willingly engaging in sexual activity. It is, therefore, the responsibility of adults to engage young people in discussions about this problem. Discussions need to portray the threat accurately and avoid the stereotypical characterization of the problem as one of violent offenders deceiving young people (Wolak et al., 2008). The real threat is not some shadowy figure pretending to be a child with candy in his hand, ready to steal away and brutalize a child; rather, the real threat is an adult preying on young people by presenting himself or herself as someone who is sympathetic, likeable, and trustworthy, and suggesting that having sex with him or her would somehow be a positive experience.

Filtering software and parental control software are often recommended as deterrents to online sexual predation. However, no filtering software can protect against all threats. Relying on software that claims to remove access to dangerous material is a risky proposition, as the filter itself can easily become an enticing challenge for young people.

Although the actual threat of sexual predation and ensnarement is different from the general public's perception, it is a serious issue—one not be taken lightly. We believe it is an adult's responsibility to take seriously any claim a child or teenager may make regarding a sexual threat and that investigation into the situation with the goal of protecting the young person is necessary. Communication is critically important in dealing with this threat; it is never something to be ignored.

For Younger Children

Keeping in mind that anyone may make use of computer-based social spaces anonymously or use a false identity, the U.S. Department of Justice (2006) recommends that elementary and middle school students understand and practice the following precautions:

- Be careful about talking to "strangers" on a computer network. Who are these people anyway? Remember that people online may not be who they seem at first.

- Never respond to messages or bulletin board items that are:

  - suggestive of something improper or indecent;

  - obscene, filthy, or offensive to accepted standards of decency;

- belligerent, hostile, combative, or very aggressive;

- threatening to do harm or danger toward you or another.

- Tell a grown-up right away if you come across any information that makes you feel uncomfortable.

- Do not give out any sensitive or personal information about yourself or your family in an Internet chat room. Be sure that you are dealing with someone you and your parents know and trust before giving out any personal information about yourself via e-mail.

- Never arrange a face-to-face meeting without telling your parent or guardian. If your parent or guardian agrees to the meeting, you should meet in a public place and have a parent or guardian go with you.

The FBI (Safety Tips, n.d.*b*) offers a similar set of recommendations:

- First, remember never to give out personal information, such as your name, home address, school name, or telephone number, in a chat room or on bulletin boards.

- Also, never send a picture of yourself to someone you chat with on the computer without your parent's permission.

- Never write to someone who has made you feel uncomfortable or scared.

- Do not meet someone or have them visit you without the permission of your parents.

- Tell your parents right away if you read anything on the Internet that makes you feel uncomfortable.

- Remember that people online may not be who they say they are. Someone who says that "she" is a "12-year-old girl" could really be an older man.

For Adolescents

Teenagers often know more about online communication than adults. To protect a young person from predatory activity, it is the adult's responsibility to learn about these online communication tools and monitor the young person's online activity. Although adults cannot monitor every minute of a teenager's online activity, responsible adults need to maintain a dialogue that shows genuine interest in the young person's well-being and a willingness to act on his or her behalf if a threat appears.

There are differing opinions on the subject of monitoring online activity. The most proactive adults advocate limiting young people's time online and ensuring that online time is spent in a public area (for example, keeping the computer in the living room or kitchen and allowing online activity only while other family members are present). A proactive approach includes requiring a young person to share his or her passwords with parents or guardians.

Adults should be aware that they can check the history of web use on any computer. Browser software such as Internet Explorer, Firefox, and Safari allow users to review the history of use—a person can easily review which websites have been accessed (unless the user has cleared the cache).

Even though most sexual predators are not relying on public information to find ways to ensnare their victims, it is always a good idea to protect one's privacy. For those who engage in social networking using sites like Facebook or MySpace, the practice of establishing a "velvet rope" is recommended ("Set-Up a Velvet Rope," 2008):

- Pay close attention to privacy settings. Set the account so that only registered friends may access detailed information and photographs.

- When adding third-party applications to a social space account, be sure to deselect any options that might share personal information.

Reporting Computer-Based Child Exploitation

At-Risk Warning Signs

According to the National Center for Missing and Exploited Children (2008), signs that a child may be at risk or a victim of sexual predation include the following.

A child spends large amounts of time online, especially at night. Many children who fall victim to predators spend a great deal of time online, using communication tools such as instant messaging and chat rooms.

Pornography in a child's computing space. Predators often supply their potential victims with pornography as a means of opening sexual discussions and lowering the child's inhibitions.

Suspicious phone calls. A child receives telephone calls from or makes calls to men or women unknown to the rest of the family. Predators may attempt to engage in "phone sex" with children and also may seek to set up an actual meeting for a real sexual encounter. Even if a child refuses to give out his or her telephone number, predators will give out their contact information.

Suspicious mail. A child receives mail, gifts, or packages from someone the family does not know. It is common for predators to send letters and gifts to their potential victims.

Suspicious screen content. A child turns the computer monitor off or quickly changes the screen on the monitor when another person comes into the room. A child looking at pornographic images or having sexually explicit conversations does not want others to see his/her activity.

A child becomes withdrawn from family or explosive. Predators may try to alienate potential victims from their families. They may portray themselves as the only one the child can trust. A child may also become withdrawn or explosive after sexual victimization.

A child is using an online account belonging to someone else. A child may meet an offender while online at a friend's house or in the library. Most computers come preloaded with online and/or Internet software. Children may also set up free e-mail accounts that their parents/guardians cannot access without the user ID and password.

Resources for Reporting Suspected Exploitation

According to the U.S. Department of Justice (2006), the first step in reporting a crime of child exploitation is to contact a local FBI office. The FBI maintains 56 field offices in major metropolitan areas throughout the United States and Puerto Rico. The FBI maintains an interactive website that makes locating and contacting its local offices relatively easy: www.fbi.gov/contact/fo/fo.htm. There is also a toll-free number for calling in reports: 1.800. CALLFBI (225.5324).

Another resource for reporting a child exploitation crime is the National Center for Missing and Exploited Children (NCMEC, 2008), which operates www.cybertipline.com, allowing parents and children to report child pornography and other incidents of sexual exploitation by submitting an online form. The NCMEC also maintains a 24-hour hotline at 1.800.THE.LOST (843.5678) and a website at www.missingkids.com.

Summary

Television programs such as *To Catch a Predator*, advertisements sponsored by groups such as the National Center for Missing and Exploited Children, and news articles in print and on the web bring the problem of online sexual predation to everyone's attention. Worried parents often share their apprehensions and concerns with teachers and administrators, hoping that they may be able to provide more information. The initial reaction among some administrators is to close off any networked computing activity that allows students to communicate directly with people outside of the school. Communication among parents, students, and educators is essential to combat this problem. Teachers and administrators can help everyone address the realities of the problem by providing the most accurate information possible about the true nature of the threat, by providing information on how to identify behaviors that indicate a problem, and by providing recommendations for initiating discussions with young people about online predators and personal safety.

Chapter 4

Misuse of Mobile Communication Devices and Cyberbullying

A student is suspended for 40 days for posting a video on YouTube he created showing unflattering images of his teacher taken during several class periods (Shukovsky & Akhmeteli, 2007).

～

Twelve students in an undergraduate accounting class use their cell phones to receive test answers via text messaging ("High School Limits," *Associated Press*, 2002).

～

A high school student has his iPod confiscated during class, and his teacher finds answers to a test, a definition list, and notes saved among his music selections. As a result, the district decides to ban all mobile devices—including cell phones ("Schools Ban iPods," *Associated Press*, 2007).

༃

An eighth grade girl turns in classmates for stealing from her; she receives over 50 hateful text messages on her cell phone in one evening from the girls (Harmon, 2006).

༃

The Threat

The potential for misuse and abuse is clear. With the widespread availability of mobile communication devices (MCDs), students with access to these devices can engage in a variety of inappropriate and harmful activities.

Over the past decade, MCDs, such as cell phones, iPods, and personal digital assistants, have become increasingly sophisticated, widely available, and relatively inexpensive. During this same time period, news reports of students misusing these devices have increased. It is difficult to determine, however, whether students have become more brazen with what they are doing with these devices or the number of students owning these devices has led to an increase in their misuse. What is clear is that many of these incidents have been reported widely, which has brought about a high level of public attention and scrutiny regarding the use of MCDs in schools.

The major concern regarding MCDs is their ability to record, display, and distribute—through audio, video, text, or a combination of all three—what takes place in schools. This is not a new phenomenon; students have been doing this for years. What is vastly different is the ease and speed with which the recording can be done. In many cases it can be done without detection by those being recorded—students, teachers, and administrators. The second major difference is in how the recorded information can be displayed and distributed. Because most of these devices are wireless, the ability exists to display and distribute information to a potentially large audience. This often is accomplished through the Internet and cellular text messaging communication. Students regularly use social networking sites, such as MySpace, Facebook, and Xanga, as well as YouTube to post media they have created with MCDs. These sites have simplified this process by creating interfaces and tools that specifically operate on cell phones, iPods, and other MCDs.

The potential threats that exist from students having access to MCDs in schools are real. Teachers and students are being recorded at school, often without their knowledge or permission, through these devices, and the recordings are being posted on the Internet. Students are being cyberbullied during and after school. Some students are using the devices to cheat on tests. Although primarily outside school hours, students can use cell phones equipped with cameras to take their own pictures either naked or partially naked. Students then send these inappropriate pictures to others via their cell phones; this process is called sexting. Parents, teachers, and administrators need to understand how these devices work and the potential that exists for their misuse in order to take proper action to diminish the problems.

Common Misperceptions of the Threat

It is not easy to establish precisely how large the problem is. What has been estimated is the level of access that students have to MCDs. A study sponsored by the Kaiser Family Foundation (2005) titled *Generation M: Media in the Lives of 8–18 Year-Olds* found that 39% of the 2,032 students in Grades 3–12 who were surveyed reported owning a cell phone. The *Speak Up 2007* national report (Project Tomorrow, 2008) indicated that approximately 32% of the students (n=319,223) surveyed in Grades 3–5 reported having a cell phone, while 51% of the Grade 6–8 students and 68% of the Grade 9–12 students reported owning a cell phone. Additionally, approximately 20% of these students reported owning a personal digital assistant (PDA). In 2005, Dodds and Mason estimated that 200,000 children between ages 5–9 in the United States owned a cell phone. The data clearly indicate that most students have access to mobile communication devices.

One could extrapolate from this data that with the current level of student access to MCDs and with the level expected to rise each year, it is inevitable that the number of incidents of student misuse will most likely increase. This thinking, we believe, leads to a common misperception that MCDs in the hands of students— especially at school—naturally leads to unwanted student behaviors. This is not necessarily the case.

What should be noted about the reports of students misusing MCDs is that the evidence is mostly anecdotal, gathered through news stories reporting students' inappropriate use of MCDs. Our search for data that supports or disproves the pervasiveness of inappropriate behaviors of students using these devices uncovered very little research. The research (e.g., Hinduja & Patchin, 2008; Kowalski & Limber, 2007; Patchin & Hinduja, 2006; i-SAFE, 2004) that does exist and is being conducted relates specifically to the role MCDs play in cyberbullying. In addition to this research, what we found was an emerging literature base (mostly pragmatic) that supports the use of MCDs as a tool that can have a positive influence on the teaching and learning process.

The Realities of the Mobile Communication Device Threat

The realities of the MCD threat are simple and clear—students have access to MCDs and, thus, have the potential for using them in inappropriate and potentially harmful ways. Because young people often have a distinct technological edge over adults when it comes to using these devices, it is critical for parents, teachers, and administrators to take the time to educate themselves regarding how MCDs work, the capabilities that they have, and how students are using them. Understanding the realities of this threat requires a working knowledge of the technology, which will allow educators to respond to the situation appropriately before it becomes a problem.

Inappropriate Images, Audio, and Video

Many MCDs are equipped with recording devices, such as cameras, that are capable of taking still images and recording audio and video. Students can easily save these images and recordings to manipulate on a computer at a later date. In addition to the capacity to capture images and to record audio and video, many of these devices can be easily connected to the Internet. Students, often with only a push of a button, can upload their media files from MCDs directly to the web or send them directly to another cell phone. People who are part of a school environment run the risk of having their pictures taken and being recorded; these recordings can then be distributed. Another recent trend is sexting—students can use cell phones equipped with cameras to take self portraits naked or partially naked and can send these inappropriate pictures to others via their cell phones.

Cheating

Students are using iPods, cell phones, and other personal digital assistants to cheat, and they are showing a great deal of creativity in doing so. Etter (2004) writes in a *Wall Street Journal* article that "... students have stopped hiding crib sheets and whispering to their neighbors—and started swapping test answers by cell phone, camera phone, and PDA" (p. 17). Ebbeling (2008) states that students are using a variety of clever methods to cheat, such as "... dictating notes onto an iPod; photographing exam questions and seeking help from friends via text messages." It is evident that some students use MCDs to cheat; how widespread this form of cheating has become is not known.

Cyberbullying

According to the National Crime Prevention Council (2007), "Online bullying, called cyberbullying, happens when teens use the Internet, cell phones, or other devices to send or post text or images intended to hurt or embarrass another person." Several research studies have been conducted on cyberbullying that provide insights into its pervasiveness.

In 2004, i-SAFE, a nonprofit organization focusing on student Internet safety, surveyed 1,500 students throughout the United States in Grades 4–8. The data they gathered revealed the following statistics about cyberbullying:

- 42% of the students surveyed have been bullied while online. Of this group, it has happened multiple times to one out of every four.

- 35% of the students have been threatened online. Of this group, close to one out of five have been threatened more than once.

- 21% of the students indicated they have received mean or threatening e-mail or other electronic messages (e.g., text messages).

- 58% of the students admitted that someone has said mean or hurtful things to them online. Of this group, more than four out of ten indicated this has happened more than one time.

- 53% of the students admitted to having said something mean or hurtful to another person while online. Of this group, approximately one out of every three has done this more than once.

- 58% have not told their parents or another adult about something mean or hurtful that happened to them online (i-SAFE, 2004).

Hinduja and Patchin (2005) conducted a similar survey of 1,500 Internet-using adolescents. Their findings indicate that 34.4% of the students reported having been cyberbullied, and 12.5% reported that they have been threatened physically. Close to 5% reported being scared for their safety. The cyberbullying experiences took place most frequently in chat rooms (55.6%), via text messaging (48.9%), and through e-mail (28%).

In a comparable study, Kowalski and Limber (2007) surveyed 3,767 middle school students in the southeastern and north-western United States to explore the students' experiences with cyberbullying—as victims and bullies. The researchers found that 11% of the students had been victims of cyberbullying at least once in the last couple of months prior to the survey; 7% said that they were cyberbullies and victims; and 4% said they had cyberbullied at least one time in the previous couple of months prior to the survey but reported not being a victim. The most common venues (mirroring those found in the 2005 Hinduja and Patchin study) for cyberbullying were chat rooms, e-mail, and instant messaging. Kowalski and Limber (2007) report that almost half of the cyberbullying victims indicated they did not know the bully's identity.

Common Responses

In dealing with the threats of mobile communication devices in schools, the most common responses range from banning their use to the full embrace of their use as tools that can invigorate teaching and enhance student learning.

Banning or Restricting Use of MCDs

The most straightforward approach—and the most drastic—for dealing with mobile communication devices has been to ban them from schools. Numerous states, cities, and districts have implemented this approach. In 2006, New York City schools began to enforce a cell phone ban policy that had been on the books for years. Through random searches of students for weapons, when cell phones were found, they were confiscated. This policy angered many parents, who believed that the policy interfered with a "parent's right to determine a child's care, custody, and control" (Maull, 2007). Eight parents filed a lawsuit against the New York City Department of Education in July 2006, challenging the cell phone ban. Department of Education officials responded to the parents' allegations by stating that banning cell phones was a reasonable way to ensure that a safe learning environment was maintained. The New York Supreme Court upheld the city schools' decision to ban cell phones.

In suburban Chicago and in Florida, cell phone use is restricted rather than banned. Students at many suburban Chicago high schools are allowed to bring phones to school but are restricted as to when they can be used (typically before and after school). The state of Florida, during the 2007–08 school year, passed legislation that prohibited students from having cell phones or other electronic devices on them while taking the Florida Comprehensive Assessment Testing. When students were caught with any of these devices—even if the devices were turned off and in a pocket—their tests were nullified. In California, students may legally carry cell phones to schools; individual districts set policies for when students can use them.

Planned Use

At the opposite end of the spectrum from completely banning MCDs from schools is embracing them, as some districts and schools have done throughout the United States. Administrators, teachers, and support staff in these districts and schools work together to determine how the devices can be used to benefit teaching and learning. Out of numerous examples of positive student use of MCDs in the classroom, a few are the following:

- Cell phones equipped with cameras can be used to take pictures of notes a student was not able to copy during class.

- Students can text message assignments to absent students.

- Homework assignments can be recorded in PDAs to provide students with a record of what they need to complete.

- Students can use iPods to listen to practice words and phrases in a foreign language.

- Students use their cell phones as they would clickers to participate in live polls and take quizzes given by their teachers during class.

Several books and websites are available that describe effective uses of MCDs in the classroom (e.g.: Kolb, 2008; Prensky, 2004; http://teachdigital.pbworks.com).

When MCDs become part of the overall learning environment, preventive measures can be taken to help ensure that students are using the devices appropriately. Teachers can help students learn to use the devices appropriately by discussing what behaviors are allowed and not allowed, rather than banning the devices and wasting time and energy trying to catch students using them. Journalist Ian Gillespie writes in his article, "Teaching Students to Navigate Digital Diversions," that rules on the use of cell phones, iPods, and BlackBerries are necessary, but denying students the ability to use them throughout the school day is a mistake. Gillespie quotes John Barnett, an assistant professor of education at the University of Western Ontario, who specializes in online education. Barnett states, "Rather than banning these devices, we need to actually use them. We need to bring them onboard … and teach [students] the appropriate uses of these digital technologies" (2008). Marc Prensky, the futurist who coined the terms "digital native" and "digital immigrant," supports this idea. He recommends that school personnel should embrace technology like cell phones for "their educational advantage" rather than clash with students over their use (2004, p. 2). Schools should be places where students develop the skills they need to be successful in the 21st century.

Measures to Prevent Cyberbullying

Another common response is to take preventive measures.
One measure is to educate students on the potential dangers of
cyberbullying and on responsible use of MCDs. The Kamaron
Institute (2008) provides two helpful lists related to cyberbullying
that can be used to provide parents, teachers, administrators, and
students with information that can help preempt cyberbullying.
The first list, designed specifically for parents, also is appropriate for
administrators and teachers:

- Install filtering and blocking software on all computers.
  Understand, however, that being proactive is the only real
  deterrent and the best resource for bullying preemption.

- Keep your computer(s) in easily viewable places.

- Model the behavior you want to see in your child.

- Talk regularly with your child about online activities he or she
  is involved in.

- Set firm guidelines for cell phone and other MCD use, and
  monitor that behavior.

- Talk specifically about cyberbullying. Explain that it is harmful
  and unacceptable behavior.

- Outline your expectations for responsible online behavior and
  clearly explain the consequences for inappropriate behavior.

- Encourage your child to tell you immediately if he or she is a
  victim of cyberbullying.

- Tell your child not to respond to a bully.

- Stay calm. Plan in advance how you will calmly receive the news that your child is being bullied and the solution steps you will take. You will want the evidence. Tell your child to save the bullying messages or photo.

- Call your child's school. Ask the principal what measurable, bullying preemption, activity-based programs the school has in place. Offer to serve on the group that expands the school's behavior policies to include cyberbullying, as it disrupts the school's teaching and learning environment:

This list is designed for students with tips for dealing with cyberbullying:

- Tell a trusted adult about the bullying, and keep telling about it until the adult takes action.

- Don't open or read messages by cyberbullies.

- Tell your school if the cyberbullying is school related. Many schools have a bullying solution in place.

- Don't erase the messages—they may be needed to take action.

- Protect yourself—never agree to meet with the person or with anyone you meet online.

- If you are bullied through a chat room or instant messaging, the "bully" can often be blocked.

- If you are threatened with harm, inform the local police.

Additionally, administrators and teachers should be aware of the laws and policies that exist regarding cyberbullying. These are often tied to current anti-bullying laws and policies. Although there is not a national cyberbullying law, as of early 2009, more than a dozen states had passed laws and policies on cyberbullying; they include Arkansas, Delaware, Idaho, Iowa, Michigan, Minnesota, Nebraska, New Jersey, Oklahoma, Oregon, South Carolina, and Washington (Surdin, 2009).

Recommendations

The following recommendations can be used as starting points to help teachers and administrators effectively deal with the potential threats of MCDs.

Awareness and Knowledge

Exercising professional responsibility regarding the threat of mobile communication devices begins with administrators and teachers having an awareness and understanding of these devices and their capabilities. Students are clearly drawn to MCDs. The research shows (e.g., *Speak Up 2007* and *Generation M: Media in the Lives of 8–18 Year-Olds*) that students have access to and use these devices; this trend will continue. Teachers should experiment with MCDs as learning tools. Numerous resources are available—many free ones on the web—that can provide teachers with examples and ideas on how to integrate MCDs into the classroom. The more a teacher knows about MCDs, the better equipped he or she will be to minimize the threats associated with them.

Policies

To mitigate the potential threats associated with MCDs, schools have begun to develop policies that provide guidelines on how MCDs are to be integrated into the school environment. If policies do not exist, administrators should work to develop them. Policies range from a full embrace of MCDs to exploit their capabilities as potential learning devices to a complete ban of MCDs. Most schools, however, have taken a middle ground that allows MCDs at school to be used for specific purposes and during specific times. Teachers should be aware of these policies (including state laws and policies, particularly if they are teaching in a state listed in the previous section) because they interact with students continuously throughout the school day and are in a position to influence students' behavior in positive ways.

Student Education and Understanding

A major threat students face as a result of MCDs is cyberbullying. Although this threat has been around since the early days of the Internet, it has become more prevalent with the proliferation of MCDs. It is extremely important that students are educated not only on the consequences of violating anti-bullying policies, but also on how to make sure that cyberbullying does not occur. Parents and teachers play a crucial role in educating students about cyberbullying—what it is, how to prevent it, and what to do if it happens.

Parent Involvement

Including parents and other educational and community stake-holders in the conversation about how MCDs will or will not be used in schools can help to ease parents' fears. The conversations can occur through synchronous and asynchronous means, such as at an open house, during parent-teacher conferences, through school districts' websites, and via newsletters sent to students' homes. Parents may need to be educated regarding how MCDs function and what their potential threats may be as well as the realities of the threats. Schools can go a long way toward gaining parents' support by being open and transparent about MCD policies and their implementation.

Summary

The inappropriate use of mobile communication devices has been widely publicized. Some young people have used the devices to engage in harmful activities against others (e.g., publicizing embarrassing recordings made at school, cyberbullying) and against themselves (e.g., sexting and cheating). One of the most common reactions to the inappropriate use of MCDs is to ban them completely from schools. Although this reaction may seem like the most logical solution, it is often not in the best interests of students, parents, and teachers. Mobile communication devices serve practical purposes and ever-increasing academic purposes. Education and communication are key elements to help ensure that the devices are used appropriately. Students should understand the dangers of using MCDs, and parents should be aware of the potential dangers involved in their use, such as cyberbullying. Teachers should be allowed to exercise professional responsibility to determine when and how the devices are integrated into the classroom. Rather than banning them, districts and schools should develop policies that clearly outline their positive uses and the consequences for their misuse. Administrators, teachers, parents, and students should come together to discuss the issues to help design policies that are well thought out and that do not bring about unintended consequences, which can hamper innovation in the classroom.

Chapter 5

Network Security vs. Access

Thirty students met during a school lunch break with their laptops. Students continuously hit their F5 keys, which refreshed a web page—completely devouring the school's Internet bandwidth. This process broke through the school's network filter, allowing students to view pornographic websites (Carter, 2008).

ॐ

A computer virus disables Internet service to 36 schools in Berkeley County for several days after the failure of antivirus software ("Berkeley Schools," *Post and Courier*, 2008).

ॐ

A high school student faces 38 years in prison for tampering with his grades, altering his SAT score results, and cheating on exams after hacking into the district's network (Chueng, 2008).

✑

A high school teacher is provided with a new computer, but the computer's CD drive had been disabled due to concerns that the illegal copying of discs or the installation of programs could occur (personal communication, 2008).

✑

The Threat

The threat of disabled and hacked networks is real. Network security refers to the maintenance of any network, whether it is located at home, in a school, or in a business. There are multiple aspects of security, including keeping the computers and their accompanying hardware safe, as well as keeping them efficiently wired and functional. An additional concern relative to network security is the maintenance of data, which may contain confidential and sensitive information, and keeping all data and software protected from corruptible events and e-mail free from large amounts of spam.

Networks disabled by viruses or other malicious attacks can stop productivity, derail instruction, and freeze schools and businesses alike. Such problems are costly in terms of time and money, as troubleshooting and fixing damaged systems can be considerably labor intensive.

Common Misperceptions of the Threat

As we come to rely on computers and networks more and more, we may find ourselves increasingly concerned that a breach in security will cause significant problems for everyone. Computer network problems, such as the introduction of a new virus or programming error, combined with our popular culture's depiction of network security as a fragile condition that anyone with a little knowledge and some free time can destroy, might cause anyone to lose confidence in computing technology.

Even sophisticated computer specialists can find themselves frightened by a threat to network security, as was evident at the turn of the millennium. The Y2K scare (the concern that computing systems could not accurately interpret the year as 2000) caused some experienced information technology specialists to be worried to the point of stockpiling food and toilet tissue.

Network administrators may react to the threat by trying to "lock down" everything within their systems to avoid any tampering. The assumption is often that this is the best approach to maintain a secure environment. Teachers and students may avoid using computers for fear of inadvertently causing a problem.

Schools need networks to function, and they must be secure; it is absolutely necessary to protect computer networks from malicious attacks and theft of information. There are ways to protect networks that maximize usability and minimize threats. Unfortunately, school districts may choose to implement measures that make technology use inflexible and unappealing. When computing technology becomes less user friendly and more difficult to use for classroom instruction, it is likely to be abandoned.

The Realities of Network Security

Threats to school and district security do exist. What schools do in response to this concern is sometimes surprising. External threats such as viruses and worms can completely disable networks, corrupt data, and damage software. There is the risk of theft or access to student and staff personal information, as well as other confidential school-related information. Student hackers have tampered with grades, accessed tests and test questions, bypassed security filters, and maliciously damaged systems. With the adoption of 1-to-1 initiatives, laptops and wireless access are increasingly available in schools. In schools with wireless service, there are likely to be areas where the filtering system is weak. In such cases, district networks' security measures can be avoided by savvy students who may attempt to access areas of the network that administrators assumed to be secure.

Many concerns regarding network security are real, and damages to technological infrastructure can be costly in terms of time, money, and personal resources. Administrators, who are responsible for the general well-being of the school and district, often take very conservative approaches to securing networks. In this section, we outline some of the concerns about secure networks in hopes of extending the dialogue between information technology (IT) administrators and educators who are attempting to integrate technology into teaching and learning.

Cost

As computing technology is an incredible financial investment, a primary concern of administrators is that of cost. Nonfunctional networks slow productivity, require substantial time and expertise to fix, and result in increased costs. On the flip side is the cost of network security—in general, the more technical the solution, the higher the cost.

Sensitive and Confidential Information

School district networks often contain a variety of sensitive information, including personal information, databases of grades, and assessments of students and teachers. Breaches of confidential information can have huge political and legal ramifications for individuals and school districts, especially if personal e-mails are accessed.

Student Safety

Another area of concern often voiced by administrators is the protection and safety of students. As discussed in Chapter 4, administrators need to make sure that students are not exposed to potentially harmful content or situations while using the web. Many security measures are implemented with "student safety" as the rationale.

Teacher Access and Productivity

Administrators want teachers to be productive. To this end, some schools and districts have created virtual private networks (VPNs). A VPN allows teachers to access files and folders stored on a school network from their computers at school and at home. Teachers can work on files in the VPN in the evenings and on the weekends. To do this, a school must have an extremely secure firewall in place. An additional concern is the risk of spam inundating e-mail systems.

Access and Functionality

Teachers seek to maintain the well-being of the school and district as well as the well-being of students, other faculty members, and staff. However, teachers often express concerns about access and functionality that are specific to their professional responsibilities. To use technology effectively as an instructional tool in the classroom, teachers need efficient access both to the Internet and to school files. Efficient access requires speed as well as convenience. Although teachers may have concerns similar to administrators in terms of costs, protecting data, and student safety, teachers primarily want and need access. For many this includes being provided with server space for educational and education-related websites. Teachers want to be able to install software, utilize flash drives to transport work to and from home and between computers, and have freedom to access the Internet.

Common Responses

Network infrastructure security policies vary widely from state to state and even from district to district. Nonetheless, there are several responses that are commonly used. These include such things as restricting permissions and use, using blocks and filters, and disabling USB drives. The following section provides an overview of these common responses.

Restricting Permissions

Permissions on a computer are said to be restricted when a user is allowed to complete only certain functions. Restricted permissions can usually be overridden only with the appropriate password. There are several reasons why permissions are restricted, and there are various levels of restrictions. Restrictions can prevent a user from altering desktop settings or prevent access to certain files. Districts are frequently concerned that teachers will download software illegally or install a single program on multiple computers, violating copyright and software permissions. This fear has often resulted in complete restriction of permissions. It is not uncommon for network administrators to completely prevent teachers from installing any new software.

Blocking Instant Messaging

Concern over the misuse of the network or the content that can appear via instant messaging (IM) has resulted in the blocking of instant messaging in many school districts. Instances of students breaching network filters via IM and blogging software have been reported. Instead of trying to educate and supervise students on appropriate IM use, some districts choose disabling Web 2.0 features as the safest alternative.

Disabling of USB Drives

While businesses and organizations often worry about the illegal downloading of sensitive data, concerns over illegal downloads and file sharing of such things as MP3 files and videos have resulted in the disabling of USB ports, thus protecting against the copying of files using USB flash, jump, or thumb drives. The disabling of ports happens in a variety of ways, including the use of software that allows an administrator to write protect the drives, the use of a blocker that disables the use of removable devices like flash drives but not network-connected devices like printers, and the complete disabling of USB drives by physical means. Filling a port with epoxy has even been recommended as a means of disabling USB ports! When one of the authors of this book expressed disbelief regarding USB disabling with a school district IT administrator, the administrator's response was, "Well, you should see what messes teachers make!"

Firewalls, Antivirus, and Spam Filters

Other common security measures employed by school districts include antivirus software installed on clients' workstations at school and at home. A common measure is to install a firewall on a district's proxy server. The proxy server is the main point of entry to a district's network, and a firewall is software that regulates who enters the network via the Internet and what type of information can pass through. Firewalls include antispam software that protects the e-mail server.

Policies and Procedures

The development and dissemination of security policies and procedures (Zeltser, 2008) are generally considered an important piece of planning for network security. Security policies should include delineating a clear statement of the roles and responsibilities of network users, plans for regular network maintenance, and the implementation of security assessments. Security assessments are discussed in greater detail at the end of this chapter.

Restricting Server Use

Some schools completely disallow the use of the server for classroom websites and/or teachers' websites. Teachers are simply not allowed to upload any files or create access points to the web. In these schools, justifications for such strict policies are concerns about network security breaches, concerns about what teachers might post to the web, or worries about what teachers may do to endanger the network accidentally.

Recommendations

The question about what constitutes appropriate security measures does not have an easy answer. For many of these issues, security is the inverse of access, and there truly appears to be no "win-win" solution. Instead, IT administrators and teachers must compromise. For any compromise to be effective, both sides need to buy into the process. Failure to appreciate either the need for security or the need for access often results in counterproductive behaviors, such as IT managers disabling valuable educational resources or teachers circumventing draconian security restrictions and exposing the network to even more peril than it faced before. Wesley Fryer (2003) recommends six major areas to focus on to balance security with access:

1. Develop a network rights strategy

2. Manage, without restricting, desktop computer activity so that instructional needs are balanced with desktop security

3. Monitor student use

4. Block unauthorized access from the outside through the use of firewalls

5. Customize the firewall to meet functional requirements

6. Set up secure remote access, so that teachers can use the school server from home

Network Rights Strategies

Chapter 2 of this book contains a brief discussion on the development of acceptable use policies (AUPs). AUPs are contracts between the school and the students and between the school and the teachers that define users' actions so that all users cooperate to keep their school's network secure. These policies can educate students and teachers on how to keep the network operational and usable by all.

Balance Instructional Needs with Desktop Security

Prohibiting teachers from downloading and installing software can limit just-in-time opportunities for instruction and hinders teachers' ability to adjust for flexibility in instructional planning. Teachers need to make sure that the software being used in their classrooms is legally installed, although it is ultimately the school district's responsibility for illegal or unauthorized use of software. If a school district is found to be using unregistered or illegally installed software, the penalty can be costly. Therefore, it is reasonable for network administrators to do periodic reviews and audits of software to make sure that nothing is unregistered or has been illegally installed. Software programs called "asset management software" are available that will support network administrators in this endeavor.

Server Space and Network Use

Allowing teachers to use the web to create classroom websites and to utilize Web 2.0 technologies enhances their teaching and motivates students. Web 2.0 technology is fundamentally important to modern classroom uses of instructional technology. When district IT administrators work *with* teachers, teachers are likely to cooperate in keeping the network secure. When teachers demonstrate that they understand the IT administrators' concerns about network stability and security, both groups can work together to maintain access and flexibility on the network. Communication is key to maintaining network security and access.

Monitor Student Use

Schools frequently use software that monitors users, including computer activity at individual workstations, e-mail via the school's e-mail server, and students' and employees' use of the Internet. Teachers should be informed of appropriate educational use for themselves and their students (which most often does not include group e-mails about politics or religion, or jokes). Districts should determine whether they need to monitor teachers. We do not advocate surveillance of professional staff; we feel it conveys a lack of trust and promotes an adversarial relationship between administration and staff.

Firewalls

Prudent school districts invest in a good firewall that allows for speedy access to the Internet while blocking unwanted outside access and protecting mail servers, web servers, and media (video and audio) transmission. Districts need to educate teachers and students on risks, such as opening unknown e-mail attachments.

Security Assessments

Every school district should develop a comprehensive security assessment plan. This plan should include a review of the physical characteristics of the network, how the firewall is configured, and the knowledge of necessary security measures as well as the trustworthiness of the people who are using the network. Software tools are available to assist with these assessments, which should be done periodically. Firewall configuration needs to be free from configuration errors. The assessment should also include a review of network architecture deficiencies (Zeltser, 2008).

Included in a security assessment is a review of the security procedures and policies in place within the school district. It is important to establish regular routines to keep antivirus software continually updated and ensure that the network itself receives frequent security updates.

Secure Passwords

As teachers are often required to post grades on the school network, it is important to ensure that student access to these areas is impossible. Teachers must not leave their login information and passwords near their computers or "hidden" in their desks. Even well-hidden information can be found by savvy students. Hardened passwords (those with uppercase and lowercase letters and numbers, for example), although cumbersome because of the difficulty of remembering various configurations, are essential for allowing only teachers and administrators access to the network. Teachers should be encouraged to memorize hardened passwords.

Those who manage networks walk a fine line between maintaining security and maintaining an instructionally useful technological infrastructure. Collaboration among IT administrators, school administrators, and teachers is key to making sure that computing technologies are used to their full potential in classrooms. The ultimate purpose of incorporating technology in the classroom is the enhancement of student learning. Anything less and technology becomes an expensive waste of resources.

Chapter 6

Inappropriate Uses of the Network

Jean was excited by her new job as a middle school health teacher and was thrilled when she was given a laptop computer. However, along with the laptop came explicit directions: The laptop was not to leave the school. One afternoon when she hadn't finished planning her lessons for the next day, she decided that there wouldn't be any harm in taking the laptop home. Later that night a large bear appeared on her screen, and the computer would no longer access her home wireless connection. The next day she had to ask the IT administrator to unlock her computer. She was admonished for inappropriately using school resources (personal communication, 2008).

ॐ

The Threat

The possibility of inappropriate use exists wherever there is a computer and an Internet connection. Inappropriate use can range from sending personal e-mails, to creating a classroom-based website, to using Web 2.0 social networking applications—depending on the school district. How teachers and students are allowed to use school district technologies and which uses are defined as inappropriate vary greatly from one school district to another.

Much of the content in this chapter draws from previous chapters in this book, such as network security, protecting students, and inappropriate content. This is because districts' decisions about how a school's network should be used are based on beliefs or experiences about how networks operate, how technology should be used, and fears regarding what might happen when students and teachers go online.

The web is a powerful tool used by students, teachers, and administrators alike. Accessing the web from school requires the use of the school's network. A school's network is owned by the school district, and ultimately it is the school district that is liable for how that network is used. Determining what is appropriate and what is inappropriate use is a reasonable topic for discussion, as there are few true absolutes in how a school network should be used (except for viewing pornography or engaging in hate-based activities, which are always illegal in schools). Most school districts have policies in place that explicitly state that school computing technology and the network must only be used for educational activities. Defining the boundary between acceptable and unacceptable use is complicated and easily blurred.

Administrators have the ongoing concern of maintaining the school and district's financial well-being. This means protecting investments in infrastructure, as well as avoiding lawsuits. Most school district administrations support the use of school technology resources for the sole use of appropriate, school-related communications and activities. Inappropriate uses of a network, however they are defined, are viewed as threats to the security of students and to the financial well-being of the district, due to their potential damage to the technological infrastructure and concerns about lawsuits. Inappropriate uses of computing technologies can also interrupt the traditional schooling of students.

Common Misperceptions of the Threat

Just about everyone worries that misusing computer resources will severely reduce productivity and, in worst-case scenarios, cause students harm.

Common concerns about inappropriate network use include students being distracted from instruction through their use of instant messaging and social spaces, or worse, that these activities could foster improper and dangerous behaviors, such as cyberbullying.

Adults worry that students are communicating inappropriate content to each other through the new technologies. Administrators may worry that teachers are making inappropriate use of the network.

The Realities of Inappropriate Network Use

Real concerns do exist regarding the use of school property. One concern is related to the educational value of the activities in which students are engaged, especially regarding Web 2.0 technologies. Some educators (and parents) do not see the educational value in the use of many Web 2.0 technologies, such as instant messaging and social spaces. Furthermore, there is the real concern that students will engage in activities that are not educational, such as chatting, cyberbullying, and using school time to engage in other nonacademic activities. In contrast, many teachers see the value and power of engaging students with the use of such technologies.

Additional concerns revolve around personal use of school resources. There have indeed been instances where school employees have used the Internet during school time to view inappropriate (pornography, gambling, and hate) websites or have spent an inordinate amount of school time engaged in exchanging personal e-mails. Such abuses have created real concerns over potential lawsuits.

Personal Use of the Internet

Teachers, like most people, rely daily on the Internet and digital technologies for personal needs. Teachers bank, shop, and communicate with friends, family, and others via e-mail. The vast majority of teachers are highly committed to their students. For many, separating what happens in the classroom and at school from what is considered a personal life is difficult because they are so interconnected. Thus, it is sometimes difficult to recognize what is a school-related use of the network and what is personal. Furthermore, teachers are expected not only to keep abreast of ongoing developments in technology but also to incorporate new technologies into lessons. This required research and study can be difficult to classify as personal or professional. For example, the woman in this chapter's anecdote did not see a difference between working on the computer at school and taking it home, where she would continue to use it to complete school work. For her and for most teachers, planning lessons and projects, doing research to enhance instruction, grading papers, communicating with parents of students, and related responsibilities extend the job far beyond the contracted school day.

Web 2.0 Access

Students are using Web 2.0 technologies to do research for school assignments and to have fun whether or not their teachers are using these technologies. Students engage in social networking on sites such as MySpace and Facebook. They instant message through computers and wireless technologies, such as cell phones. They also download music and videos, engage in blogging, and play games online. Teachers who recognize the power of Web 2.0 technologies have transformed their classrooms into vibrant learning spaces where students can participate in and out of class. For example, an online blog about *A Wrinkle in Time*, a popular book by Madeleine L'Engle, is set up as an online literature circle, and ninth graders can use free wiki software to manage a collaborative research project and communicate with each other from home via instant messaging as they work on the project's components. Although limited, initial research into the effectiveness of using Web 2.0 technologies in the classroom indicates that the students who participate in Web 2.0 activities in the classroom are more engaged (Crook et al., 2008).

To use Web 2.0 technologies successfully, teachers need to have access to reliable networks, ample bandwidth, limited filters, and acceptable use policies that allow for the use of blogs, wikis, and classroom websites, as well as capability to view video and use RSS (really simple syndication) feeds.

Common Responses

School districts undertake many types of strategies to manage the appropriate use of technology. These include the development of acceptable use policies, limiting the use of Web 2.0 applications, using website filters and blocking software, using monitoring and Internet surveillance software, and restricting access to servers.

Acceptable Use Policies

An acceptable use policy (AUP) is a written contract between an Internet computer user and the school district, the school, or a classroom teacher. Almost all school districts have developed AUPs to help define how staff and students may use district technology resources. These policies generally state that school computing technologies will only be used for educational purposes. The stringencies and consequences for not following the policy vary, depending upon the culture of the school district. AUPs are discussed in more detail in Chapter 2, Acceptable Use Policies and Contracts.

Limiting Web 2.0 Use

Web 2.0 is a term that refers to the variety of aspects of the web that make it a powerful tool for socializing, collaborating, and sharing information. Web 2.0 is also called the read-write web due to the two-way flow of information. In many schools, the AUP clearly states that students and staff alike are not to use certain Web 2.0 technologies, such as blogging software, personal e-mail, social networking sites, or instant messaging, when their computers are connected to the school's server or network.

Filtering and Blocking Software

As elaborated upon in Chapter 2, districts use filtering and blocking software in an attempt to keep students safe and prevent access to inappropriate content by anyone within the school system.

Monitoring and Surveillance Software

It is not uncommon for school districts to purchase and employ software that monitors whatever information is transmitted over the district's network. This includes both e-mail transmissions and Internet access. A wide range of surveillance software is available; administrators can and often do know exactly what is happening on school computers. In some instances, reports are generated on a regular basis and can then be reviewed by IT administrators. In most cases, the accessing of inappropriate sites and other behaviors can be linked to an individual computer or an individual's log in.

Restricting Access

A common method of controlling access to the Internet is for a school district simply to "lock down" individual workstations, which can then be released only by an administrative password. In many districts, teachers are not allowed to create and store websites or to use Web 2.0 technologies.

Recommendations

Vicki Davis (2007), an award-winning classroom teacher, shares six pillars of the Web 2.0 classroom:

1. Internet safety and privacy

2. Information literacy

3. Internet citizenship

4. Internet teamwork

5. Intentional Internet activities

6. An engaged teacher

Each of Davis's pillars is addressed, although in some cases tangentially, throughout this book, along with suggestions for the necessary support that makes these pillars a reality. In all cases, teachers make it their responsibility to teach students the skills to be safe, to maintain privacy, to evaluate and respond to information on the web critically, and to engage in a responsible way with others online. At the same time, teachers protect students from harm through responsible supervision. They teach and promote interactions and positive collaborations and create intentional, carefully planned activities that foster student learning, using the Internet and Web 2.0 resources, such as wikis, blogs, social networks, and other digital technologies. These teachers are absolutely engaged in the learning, research and communication processes, and activities of the students. Such teachers must be trusted to use their district's network to the fullest extent possible. This means that school district IT staff have worked to establish networks that have enough bandwidth to accommodate heavy use and traffic with minimal filters and that teachers are trusted and trained to act as knowledgeable, engaged professionals.

Uses of school networks for illegal, illicit, or unethical activities are rare. Rules that punish or restrict teachers for doing their jobs are likely to be counterproductive. For example, the young teacher in the anecdote who was reprimanded for using her laptop at home to do school-related work will likely avoid doing extra work at home in the future. Explicit acceptable use policies go a long way toward defining roles and responsibilities of students and school employees and should be reasonable and include access to blogs, wikis, teacher- and class-created websites, and personal e-mail. Keeping in mind the unique job of teaching, various teaching styles, and the needs of teachers can help district and IT administrators devise realistic, useful AUPs. No one questions personal phone calls that are made during lunch breaks or after school. Teachers should also be allowed to take care of personal business online during breaks and before and after school as long as it does not interfere with their responsibilities. After all, teachers allow school business to come home, as they spend hours of noncontracted time working on lessons and grading papers; in addition, many teachers spend significant amounts of their own money for classroom materials and supplies.

Chapter 7

Copyright Infringement

An article in *eSchool News* reports, "When digital video first streamed into schools, many predicted it would one day revolutionize teaching and learning. But the threat of lawsuits and new copy-protection technologies are keeping educators from exercising their legal right to use portions of video and other digital media in the classroom" (Murray, 2004).

୬

CNET News reports that the media company Viacom filed a $1 billion claim against Google for copyright infringement because YouTube has unauthorized clips from Viacom's feature films and television shows on its site (Sandoval, 2008).

୬

The Recording Industry Association of America (RIAA) is actively pursuing copyright violations involving music piracy on college campus networks. ("RIAA Cracks Down," *ZDNet*, 2007).

⁊

In an article in *Education Week*, Renee Hobbs, a professor of communication at Temple University, wrote, "When teachers in a suburban-Philadelphia school district heard about the music industry's legal victory requiring a single mother from Minnesota to pay more than $220,000 for sharing 24 songs online, the news seemed to confirm their worst suspicion: It isn't safe to use digital media as a teaching tool" (Hobbs, 2008).

⁊

The Threat

Copyright infringement happens regularly, and the fear of legal repercussions affects decisions in the classroom. Within the last decade, teachers have become much more aware of copyright issues and have expressed greater concern about copyright infringement. Many teachers have become fearful of using materials they did not create themselves.

Infringement may occur any time intellectual property owned by one person or group is used without the owner's permission. Intellectual property may be defined as material created and expressed in tangible form, including works of art, books, magazine articles, and audio or video recordings.

The probable cause for the increase in concern over copyright is the relative ease with which copyrighted items may be copied and distributed. Digital media, including music, images, and video, may be duplicated infinitely without any loss of quality, and this media may be distributed practically around the world with the touch of a button.

Common Misperceptions of the Threat

Teachers, aware of copyright law, often fear penalty, censure, and public embarrassment resulting from copyright infringement.

Copyright holders, represented by such groups as the Recording Industry Association of America (RIAA), are concerned that they will not profit from their own creations. Media portrayal of businesses and organizations aggressively prosecuting copyright infringement has caused many educators to avoid duplication of any copyrighted material. Teachers and administrators have nightmare visions of corporate lawyers descending upon their schools or upon them individually and engaging in expensive and publicly embarrassing lawsuits over misuse of copyrighted material.

Conversely, many educators misinterpret the "fair use" doctrine, assuming that as long as the copyrighted material is being used in an educational setting, the educator is exempt from copyright infringement laws.

In their study, "The Cost of Copyright Confusion for Media Literacy," researchers Renee Hobbs, Peter Jaszi, and Pat Aufderheide (2007) write:

> In K–12, higher education, and after-school programs and workshops, teachers face conflicting information about their rights, and their students' rights, to quote copyrighted material. They also confront complex, restrictive copyright

policies in their own institutions. As a result, teachers
use less effective teaching techniques, teach and transmit
erroneous copyright information, fail to share innovative
instructional approaches, and do not take advantage of new
digital platforms. (p. 1)

To avoid the issue of copyright altogether, many teachers feign
ignorance, hoping to go about the business of teaching without
having to delve deeply into copyright law or discover that they
may not use the materials that work well for their students. This
approach, however, leads to an environment that may increase
instructors' anxiety about using copyrighted materials (Hobbs et al.,
2007).

The Realities of Copyright Infringement

A person found guilty of copyright infringement may be found
responsible for actual or statutory damages to the owner of the
copyright. The owner may be awarded actual damages that
are essentially recovery of any profits lost or awarded statutory
damages. Statutory damages between $500 and $20,000 for a single
infringement may be awarded depending upon the court's decision.
In the case that copyright infringement is willfully committed,
the court may award up to $100,000 in damages. The minimum
award of damages is $200 if the court finds copyright infringement
occurred (U.S. Copyright Office, 2009a).

Copyright issues are primarily civil cases. The person infringing
is sued but not charged with a crime (Templeton, 2008). This
means the copyright holder must take it upon himself or herself
to bring suit against the infringer, which is a costly and time-
consuming process. The copyright holder may well undertake the
suit if he or she is losing profits based on the infringement. In those

instances when a copyright infringement suit is filed, a judge must determine whether copyright infringement has occurred. If the judge determines copyright infringement has occurred, the judge determines the amount of damages owed to the copyright holder by the infringer.

Judges make use of a doctrine known as "fair use" when determining whether copyright infringement has occurred in educational settings. The fair use doctrine is a set of guidelines devised by federal court judges more than 150 years ago. Although it is often discussed and cited, most teachers cannot provide a working definition of what fair use actually is (Hobbs et al., 2007).

What Is Copyright?

Copyright in the United States is a form of protection based upon the principles established by the U.S. Constitution. Specific laws protect the rights of anyone who creates "original works of authorship fixed in a tangible medium of expression" (U.S. Copyright Office, 2006). Copyright law protects both published and unpublished works. Here are some examples:

- The copyright for Mickey Mouse movies is owned by the Walt Disney Company.

- The copyright for Spider-Man comics is owned by Marvel Characters, Inc.

- The copyright for the song "Happy Birthday to You" is claimed by the Warner Music Group.

An individual or group holds copyright to intellectual property as soon as it is created. One does not need to register a work with the U.S. Copyright Office in order to secure copyright for one's work

(U.S. Copyright Office, 2008). At one time, copyright notice (the word copyright or its symbol, ©, and year the work was created appearing on or next to a work) was required to maintain copyright, but that is no longer required under U.S. law.

Copyright is not transferred to a person who purchases a copy of the work. For example, owning a copy of a book does not transfer copyright to the book's owner. The owner of the book has purchased the right to read the work, and the book's owner may give or sell the book itself to another person; however, the book's owner may not legally copy and distribute the book's contents.

Copyright does not last forever; it expires over time. Copyright expires for one of three reasons: (1) 70 years have passed after the creator's death, (2) 95 years have passed since publication of an item that was made for hire or published pseudonymously or anonymously, or (3) 120 years have passed since the creation of the work. When copyright has expired, the work is considered part of the public domain; anyone may use or distribute the work.

What is not protected by copyright? According the U.S. Copyright Office (2008), several types of work cannot be copyrighted. These include the following:

- Works that have not been fixed in a tangible form of expression (e.g., speeches or performances that have not been written or recorded)

- Titles, names, short phrases, and slogans; familiar symbols or designs; variations of typographic ornamentation, lettering, or coloring; listings of ingredients or contents

- Ideas, procedures, methods, systems, processes, concepts, principles, discoveries, or devices, as distinguished from a description, explanation, or illustration

- Works consisting entirely of information that is common property, containing no original authorship (e.g.: standard calendars, height and weight charts, tape measures and rulers, and lists or tables taken from public documents or other common sources)

What is fair use? According to the U.S. Copyright Office (2009a), exclusive rights to intellectual property have limitations, and "... use by reproduction in copies or phonorecords or by any other means specified by that section, for purposes such as criticism, comment, news reporting, teaching (including multiple copies for classroom use), scholarship, or research, is not an infringement of copyright."

In determining whether fair use applies to a particular case, a judge considers the following factors:

- Whether use is of a commercial nature or is for nonprofit educational purposes

- The nature of the copyrighted work itself

- The amount used and the importance of that amount in relation to the copyrighted work as a whole

- The effect of the use upon the potential market for or value of the work. (U.S. Copyright Office, 2009a)

The fair use doctrine is a set of guidelines that court judges make use of to determine whether copyright infringement has occurred.

It is important to keep in mind that these are guidelines and not a specific formula; only a court judge may determine whether copyright infringement has occurred or if the work is being used fairly; this happens only if a suit is brought by the copyright owner.

The TEACH Act

The Technology, Education and Copyright Harmonization (TEACH) Act, signed by President George W. Bush in 2002, is an attempt to provide clarification and greater latitude for use of copyrighted materials by educators in networked computing settings. The TEACH Act allows educators working in accredited nonprofit education settings to make use of copyrighted materials for the purpose of instruction (Copyright Clearance Center, 2005).

The use of copyrighted materials must be limited to the number of students enrolled in a specific class and does not include rights to distribute textbook materials or other materials students would typically purchase. It also does not allow use of copyrighted materials for which the owners have expressly forbidden copy or redistribution. This holds true even when students access course materials through a password-protected site (e.g., signing in to a course using Blackboard).

Linking Rights

Novice web page creators sometimes wonder whether it is permissible to put links to other websites on their own pages. The traditional view among most web developers is that linking to other web pages and sites is the same as citing and referencing the works of others, which is not covered by copyright law. It is often argued that linking information is the whole point of the web. In the last ten years, however, there have been cases where judges have ruled in favor of the plaintiff regarding the inclusion of unauthorized links (Awdeh & Esquenet, 2007).

Common Responses

Many school districts provide guidelines for making use of copyrighted material. The majority of these guidelines refer people to federal and state copyright codes that can be confusing. While much of the code indicates what material is or is not copyrightable, copyright infractions are often purposefully less defined, serving as a set of guidelines that are open to interpretation on a case-by-case basis. A significant number of districts also provide specific and often very strict guidelines along with examples of how to work with copyrighted material. The goal of these strict guidelines seems to be to approach the problem from a better-safe-than-sorry angle, but overly strict guidelines may cause more problems than they solve.

Many teachers avoid using images, music, or video altogether for fear of violating copyright, while some teachers rely on the fair use doctrine as if it offered educators complete protection from prosecution. In either case, the result is the teacher taking on the role of self-professed expert regarding what media is and is not usable in an educational setting.

Recommendations

You get permission to use somebody else's work by asking for it. If you know who the copyright owner is, you may contact the owner directly. If you are unsure about the ownership or have questions about use, you may ask the U.S. Copyright Office to conduct a search of its records, or you may conduct a search yourself (www. copyright.gov/records).

Asking for permission, however, is not the same as receiving permission. In many cases the copyright holder will grant permission when asked whether the work may be used for educational purposes. In some cases the copyright holder may charge a fee for use of the copyrighted work, and in some cases the copyright holder may refuse to grant permission. If you do not receive permission to use a copyrighted work, you might consider using a similar work that is in the public domain or royalty-free material.

Using Work in the Public Domain

Items that are not protected by copyright are considered to be in the public domain. An item in the public domain may be used by anyone because no one holds copyright on that item. In the United States, copyrighted works become part of the public domain 70 years after the creator's death, 95 years after an item was made for hire or published pseudonymously or anonymously, or 120 years after the creation of the work (U.S. Copyright Office, 2008).

Using Royalty-Free Materials

Collections of images, videos, sounds, and music that may be used without paying royalties or extra fees are available for purchase. These are often referred to as "royalty-free" materials. These materials are not in the public domain, but the purchase of the collection entitles the purchasers to use the materials freely as long as they are not reselling the materials themselves (e.g., a teacher may use a royalty-free image of an apple to decorate a web page on nutrition, but the teacher may not grant use of that apple image to others).

The purpose of copyright is to allow the creator of a work to benefit from his or her creation. Just as we would not allow students to copy the work of others in a classroom and call it their own, we have to be careful not to suggest, inadvertently or otherwise, that someone else's work is ours.

It is important to keep in mind that copyright in the United States is a complicated issue. Teachers' use of copyrighted materials for presentations that they place on the Internet, such as class-related web pages, can be interpreted differently by different people (Johnson & Lamb, 2007).

In considering copyright, an important thing to keep in mind is that American copyright law attempts to balance the need to protect authors—in order to encourage people to produce original works by supporting their ability to benefit from those works—while allowing public access to original works to "maintain a democratic and educated society" (McCord Hoffman, 2001, p. 3). Copyright is not intended to close off all communication about intellectual property without the copyright owner's permission. In other words, copyright is not meant to stifle the creativity of others, including the creative act of commenting on or modifying copyrighted material. An old example is that of Mighty Mouse, a cartoon character based on Superman: Copyright law does not protect the owners of Superman from having others make creative use of the essential concept of the Superman character.

When exercising fair use, one is still responsible for providing a notice of copyright (U.S. Copyright Office, 2009a). The general rule to follow is always give credit where credit is due. When using all or part of another's work, provide copyright information about the work, and provide some means of finding the original, full work.

The safest course of action is to ask permission and provide attribution. Always ask permission to use copyrighted material, and request permission to link to other websites. Once permission is obtained, always provide attribution, explaining who created the material or who owns the material, the copyright date, title of the work, and publisher's name.

Fair use guidelines allow for the limited use of copyrighted material for purposes of commentary and criticism (NOLO, 2008). For educators this allows for use of portions of copyrighted materials for purposes of classroom instruction that are finite in duration. For example, a teacher may copy and distribute a poem she found in a magazine to her class one time (it might be a poem that addresses a current event or something relevant to a specific event within her classroom). However, if the teacher plans to use this poem year after year with students, she must obtain permission from the copyright holder. The use of copyrighted materials must be limited to the number of students enrolled in a specific class and does not include rights to distribute textbook materials or other materials students would typically purchase. It also does not allow use of copyrighted materials for which the owners have expressly forbidden copy or redistribution (Copyright Clearance Center, 2005).

Internet communications make copyright and fair use more problematic for educators. Because something like a web page is not limited to one classroom, even if it is intended as a resource only for members of that class, fair use guidelines do not necessarily apply because the copyright holders may be put in jeopardy of losing revenue or recognition for their work. Although many teachers think putting something on a classroom web page is similar to putting that item on a classroom bulletin board, in terms of copyright it is probably best to consider items placed on a web page the same way one would consider putting that item on a city billboard. The TEACH Act helps with this, but it is intended for material that can be accessed by students only, not material accessible to the general public.

The authors of *The Cost of Copyright Confusion for Media Literacy* (Hobbs et al., 2007), a report on their investigation into copyright's effect on media literacy education, recommend that educators develop a comprehensive code of practice regarding the use of copyrighted materials for instructional purposes. Although writing a comprehensive code may be beyond any one person's or single school's capability, it is a good idea to determine a set of guidelines for use before a problem arises. Using the fair use doctrine and the TEACH Act as starting points, a basic code for teachers and students could be an excellent instructional activity of its own.

Summary

Sensational cases, such as Viacom's billion-dollar claim against Google or the Minnesota woman ordered to pay $220,000 for sharing songs online, cause a great deal of concern. No one wants to be responsible for a lawsuit, and it may seem the best way to deal with the problem is to avoid using any copyrighted materials at all. However, it would be a great tragedy if educators and schools simply stopped using all copyrighted materials; this would go against the fundamental premise of the federal copyright code. Most copyright holders are willing to give teachers and students permission to use portions of their work in educational settings, as long as the activity does not compromise the copyright holder's ability to profit from the work. To avoid misunderstandings and legal entanglements, educators should continue to learn about copyright law and engage in discussion with colleagues and students about the importance of asking permission before using work owned by another person and giving credit to the originator or owner of the work whenever portions of that work are used.

Chapter 8

Data and Identity Theft

A school district's unsecured server exposes confidential data online for approximately 7,500 students in Indianapolis ("District Posts," *eSchool News*, 2007).

✍

Approximately 40,000 former and current Chicago Public School employees' social security numbers were compromised when two laptop computers containing this information were stolen from district headquarters ("Laptop Theft," *eSchool News*, 2007).

✍

Middle school students in Virginia have their social security numbers printed on their school identification card rather than their student numbers (Anderson, 2006).

ೖ

The Threat

The threat is clear. Staff and student data are increasingly vulnerable due to school data being available in a digital format—often through networked environments.

The need to make data-driven, timely decisions has led states, districts, and schools to make student and staff data available in digital formats that are often available through network-connected databases. Although there are benefits to having data available digitally, there are serious drawbacks. One of the major drawbacks is the susceptibility of the data to being compromised by falling into the wrong hands through unintentional or intentional events, such as those described in this chapter's anecdotes.

Data Theft

Data theft is the intentional act of illegally obtaining confidential information about an individual or entity such as a school. Data theft typically does not end with obtaining confidential information only; often, stolen data is manipulated or distributed or both. The person committing data theft can come from within or outside the school environment. One such method used to steal data within an organization is through the use of portable storage devices, such as a thumb drive (also called a flash drive) or an iPod—this method of theft is called "thumb sucking" or "pod slurping" (named after the device used and the act of sucking out or slurping out data from a computer). The low cost and small size of portable storage devices have made it much easier for thieves to steal data without being noticed, even in semisupervised areas. In addition to these methods, another common method a person can use to steal school data is to hack into a school's database, as many school and district databases are accessible through the Internet.

Data theft is carried out for a variety of reasons. Disgruntled employees could decide to commit data theft after the district or school terminates their employment. Individuals could hack into a district or school computer system that is accessible through the Internet to steal staff members' personal information. Students could commit data theft by accessing school data to view and change recorded grades.

Although this chapter focuses on theft of digital data, data theft can also occur when data is available in analog format (printed reports). It is also important to note that data theft can occur and has occurred as a result of negligence. One such case happened when a university researcher inadvertently posted information about students on a publicly accessible website. In doing so, the researcher exposed student data to anyone who might have visited the site. In this case, student data could have been stolen before the site was removed from public view ("District Posts," 2007).

Identity Theft

Identity theft is a type of data theft in which a person illegally obtains information about an individual in order to gain some type of benefit; typically, the benefit is for financial gain. The information obtained that allows for identity theft often includes an individual's full name, maiden name, address, date of birth, and social security number. Access to this information allows a person almost endless possibilities for abuse. A person with this information can access protected areas of online databases, such as bank accounts, credit card accounts, and credit reports—resulting in new lines of credit opened, purchases made on credit cards, and money withdrawn from bank accounts. In some cases, the data is sold to others rather than used by the person who stole the data.

Common Misperceptions of the Threat

We frequently hear or read news about some type of data being compromised. The perception, real or not, that personal information is at risk is brought about by the national exposure the incidents receive. Several incidents over the past five years of student and staff data being stolen through various methods have occurred. However, the exact number of incidents is difficult to determine because there is not a systematic method for reporting such incidents to the public. When thefts of personal data are discovered, they are usually reported directly to those who have been affected (those who have had their personal information compromised; in the case of minors, reports would be given to their parents or guardians) and to those who are responsible for the data (such as school board members, administrators, teachers, and staff—especially technology support personnel). Only when data theft is committed on a large scale does the national media hear of the incident and report it to the public. This type of media exposure can lead to serious ramifications for a district, school, and its administrators.

One thing is clear—the reported incidents clearly highlight the threats that exist regarding the vulnerability of data in schools and the impact that data theft can have. These reported incidents often heighten awareness about data theft and the potential threats that exist with staff and student data, bringing with it public misperceptions that these incidents take place more often than they really do and that schools and districts are unprepared to protect data.

The Realities of the Threat

The reality of this threat is that it can and does occur. When it does, it can have a tremendous impact on any organization. For a business, data theft often results in proprietary information about products, marketing strategies, and strategic operations being shared with competitors. For a school, where a preponderance of data stored is about students and staff, data theft can lead to personal and confidential information being widely exposed and used maliciously. It is important for teachers and administrators to be keenly aware of the risk of data theft because they have a fiduciary obligation to protect student data.

Data theft can place schools in violation of state and federal laws designed to protect student privacy. Administrators and teachers must take the time to understand their obligations and responsibilities based on these laws. Administrators, in particular, could be held primarily responsible for any data theft that occurs. The Family Educational Rights and Privacy Act (FERPA), the Protection of Pupil Rights Amendment (PPRA), the National School Lunch Act (NSLA), and the Individuals with Disabilities Education Act (IDEA) are major examples of federal laws that dictate how student data is to be treated. In examining state law, California, for example, has several laws in addition to federal laws that specify how student data must be treated. California Education Code 60641 and the Individual Privacy Act (IPA) California Civil Code 1798.24 are two such laws (California Legislative Analyst's Office, 2008).

Common Responses

Schools will always need to collect and manage student data—especially in the current age of accountability with its heavy emphasis on standardized test scores and on the requirement to document school improvement. As technology provides for collecting and managing student data through networked environments, the need to protect private data from being stolen has brought about multiple responses. These responses often include computer and network security measures, data encryption, data access limitations, and staff training.

Computer and Network Security

The threat to computer and network security and the various responses to maintaining the security of these systems were discussed in detail in Chapter 6 of this book. Nevertheless, these issues are important enough to discuss again because of the impact these systems have on school data security. Secure computer and network systems help ensure that school data is safe. The two major goals of these responses are (1) to limit unauthorized access to computer and network systems to protect school data and (2) to keep computers and networks running smoothly to ensure that important school operations function without interruption. Examples of the solutions that help meet these goals are the following:

- Restricting permissions as to what can be done by whom on school computers and networks, such as installing software and having access to web servers

- Installing protective software, such as firewalls, virus protection software, and e-mail spam filters

- Blocking the use of various software tools, such as instant messaging and social networking sites

- Disabling USB drives on computers that contain sensitive information to prohibit use of portable digital storage devices for purposes of copying that information

A combination of these responses can contribute toward keeping schools' computer and network systems secure from malicious attacks and unintentional actions, helping to secure school data and prevent data theft. However, a consequence of these restrictions is that teachers may be limited in their access to technology. They could be shut out from using instructional software, accessing instructional websites, and accessing research or student data in a timely manner or, in some cases, at any time at all.

Data Encryption

Another response schools have undertaken is to secure data through encryption. Data encryption is the process of transforming plain text (data that anyone can read) to ciphertext (data that can be read only by an individual with a secret decryption key) (Yang, Wong, Huang, & Deng, 2007). Sophisticated data encryption techniques can be accomplished quite effectively using computers. Computer software exists that allows an individual to encrypt a document when it is being saved. This process protects the document even if it were to be stolen because the individual opening the stolen document would see the ciphertext rather than the original plain text of the document. It is possible for a person who has stolen data to decrypt an encrypted document; however, this requires a great deal of skill that only a select number of people possess.

Data encryption is also used on websites that collect and transmit data. E-commerce sites, in particular, use various methods to encrypt data gathered from customers because of the sensitive nature of the data they collect (such as credit card numbers, addresses, and phone numbers). Because school districts' data is often accessed through networked environments at schools or a central location in a district office, data encryption is essential. Districts must ensure that secure website protocols are being used to transmit data through the Internet. District and school IT personnel should understand these protocols and ensure they are functioning properly.

Data Access

A multifaceted response often used in educational settings to secure data is limiting access to data. When working in a school, it may seem as if access to school data is possible by anyone working at the school—from administrators to teachers to front office personnel. Although this perception may not be completely true, school data is often relatively easy to access. While it is important for various personnel to have access to data, it is equally important that access to students' data be limited in order to protect the data and students' privacy. Limiting access to data can be done in numerous ways. Some of the most common methods are the following.

User profiles. Setting up user profiles on computer and network systems to indicate the level of access to data that an individual has can allow IT personnel to track a user's actions when the user accesses data. It can be determined where the user accessed the systems, what data was accessed, and the actions taken on the data (such as making changes to the data, saving data, deleting data).

Strict protocols. All computer and network systems should require usernames and passwords to access data and require strict protocols for creating and using passwords. These passwords should not be shared. Policies should be in place for frequently updating the passwords. In addition, especially with school-owned laptops, passwords should be used to enable their operation. Many schools—especially universities—incorporate an added level of security to laptops by requiring a hard drive password to be entered when the laptop is booted. This is in addition to the typical username and password most schools require.

Firewalls. Installing firewalls will monitor and block user traffic on computer and network systems. Numerous commercial firewall software programs exist that are developed specifically for schools (Carter, 2008).

Restricting digital copying. Limiting or prohibiting the use of portable digital storage devices, such as thumb drives, iPods, and mini hard drives can be done by prohibiting these devices from the school or by a more extreme measure (as described in Chapter 6) of plugging up USB drives and disabling optical drives on school computer systems. Some schools have also prohibited staff from using laptops and other wireless Internet devices at school.

Tracking equipment. Installing tracking devices and passwords on school-owned equipment can help recover stolen equipment, such as laptops, that may have sensitive data stored on them ("With PC Tracking Software," 2002; Schwartz, 2008).

Again, the various solutions described serve the purpose of limiting access to sensitive data. It is important to note that these responses, although quite effective, do bring about consequences that may not be intended. For example, limiting the use of portable digital storage devices can seriously hamper a teacher's ability to bring in media that may be highly appropriate for instructional purposes. Additionally, setting up and maintaining multiple user profiles may require significant IT support. All of the responses described have associated costs involved, which administrators will have to take into consideration. While sensible security measures are necessary and prudent, others can have the proverbial effect of throwing the baby out with the bath water; in such cases, the "baby" can be several computers' permanently damaged USB ports or preventing teachers' access to educational technology in districts that overreact to threats and fears.

Staff Training

Educating employees on how to protect student data is a common and necessary response (Devaney, 2007). Staff must understand how to handle sensitive data properly. Staff development should be provided at the beginning of every year that focuses on the legal aspects regarding data, including staff responsibilities and obligations for data collection, use, and dissemination. Additionally, staff development should include training on how to use school computer and network systems properly. Staff should understand what they are allowed and not allowed to do—and what the consequences are for violating school regulations. An acceptable use policy (AUP) is a document that outlines these regulations and consequences. All schools should have an AUP in place. Often, districts create a standard AUP that covers all school employees and another AUP that students sign in order to use school computer and network systems.

Recommendations

Schools are no different than other organizations when it comes to data theft. Schools are vulnerable to having data stolen. As we discussed, it is difficult to determine the extent to which data theft is a problem in schools because there is no single agency in place that records the number and veracity of incidents schools actually encounter. Despite this, protecting data is critically important.

Staff Understanding of Responsibilities

Due to the vulnerability of the data schools collect and manage, it is crucial that school personnel exercise professional responsibility when handling student and staff data. Exercising professional responsibility begins with handling data as if it were one's own personal information. Education and training are also important. School personnel must have a clear understanding of the state and federal laws that dictate how personal information is treated. The primary responsibility rests with administrators to understand regulations about how personal data needs to be treated in order to pass this information along to staff clearly. Teachers also have the responsibility of teaching students about the dangers of data and identity theft.

Technology Plan

Administrators need to have a technology plan (that goes beyond an AUP) in place that includes data security. This plan often is developed by a committee of district personnel and is, therefore, something that an administrator adheres to rather than develops on his or her own. It is wise for administrators to be aware of the data being collected, how the data are being stored, how the data can be accessed, and who has access to various types of data. Administrators need to understand the technological precautions that are in place to maintain security of data.

Administrators should know how school data may be vulnerable and find out how security is being addressed. Administrators need to discuss these procedures with key personnel, such as IT coordinators. Specifics that were discussed in this chapter and in Chapter 6—such as restricting access to data and data encryption—should be procedures and policies that are part of an overall data security plan. The bottom line for any administrator is to be informed. Well-informed administrators ensure that policies and procedures to protect students and staff data are in place and are followed.

Chapter 9

Exercising Professional Responsibility

Educators as Decision Makers

Threats to security are real, but they need to be placed into perspective. As educators in the 21st century, we must balance the need for the protection of our students and our tools with the need for accessible and flexible applications of technology. We must find ways to encourage comfortable, safe use of computing tools and innovative technologies. We also must empower our students and ourselves to integrate these tools and technologies into classroom settings in ways that are safe and satisfying for students and teachers.

Exercising professional responsibility is critically important in creating safe and useful learning environments for students and teachers. Administrators and teachers must take leadership positions in the decision-making process. It is tempting to delegate all responsibility for security policies to information technology staff. However, administrators and teachers should take a proactive approach, working with IT personnel to develop solutions that are effective and reasonable.

Good judgment is critically important. When considering how to deal with security threats, teachers and administrators must weigh the instructional value of the technology against the severity of the threat. The first step in developing effective and reasonable safeguards is learning the true nature of each threat. Issues of sexual predation, for example, may be frightening to consider; however, by studying the data on what usually occurs, as opposed to taking actions based on fear, educators, students, and parents can develop effective preventive measures. Copyright issues may be confusing, yet educators can find ways to understand and adhere to copyright law to make best use of intellectual property for the greater good.

Being professionally responsible requires administrators and teachers to become as well-informed as possible and to take an active role in decision-making processes in their schools and districts. Reviewing the perceptions and realities of the technology-oriented security threats presented in the preceding chapters is an excellent place to begin. Educators must be sensitive to the perception of the threat in order to engage students and parents in meaningful discussion. At the same time, we need to discover the realities of the threat and then develop and enact appropriate safety measures based on facts.

Being professionally responsible also means learning as much as possible about how the technology itself works. The majority of young people may always have an advantage over most adults in terms of interest in the newest technologies and time available to become proficient in their use, but this should not be taken as an invitation for adults to abdicate responsibility for knowing how the tools work and what dangers they may pose. Experimenting with new technologies is a professional responsibility, and knowing how these technologies work is an important part of knowing what to recommend in terms of their use in the classroom.

Being professionally responsible requires considering legal issues involving inappropriate content (Chapter 2), predators or ensnarement (Chapter 3), misuse of MCDs and cyberbullying (Chapter 4), network security and inappropriate uses of the network (Chapters 5 and 6), infringement of copyright (Chapter 7), and data and identity theft (Chapter 8).

Dealing with Legal Issues

Throughout this book we have discussed various threats related to technology use in schools. When potential threats become realities, there are specific laws and regulations that affect administrators and teachers and, in some cases, students as well. This section highlights these laws and regulations, which have been mentioned in previous chapters. The following discussion is not meant to be a comprehensive examination of all existing legal issues related to technology in education—nor is it meant to provide legal advice. Our purpose is to provide an overview of major legal issues that need to be considered when dealing with potential technology threats.

Inappropriate Content

It is nearly impossible to protect students at all times from accessing and viewing inappropriate content while using technology. Despite this, the Children's Internet Protection Act of 2000 made it a requirement that schools adopt policies to protect students from inappropriate content on the Internet if they wanted to receive federal E-rate funding, a program that makes telecommunication and digital technology more affordable for schools and libraries that meet certain criteria (CIPA, 2001). The safeguards that schools must include are such things as an Internet safety policy and measures that block or filter Internet access to pictures that are obscene, are child pornography, or are harmful to minors.

Senate Bill S. 1492: Broadband Data Improvement Act, was passed by the 110th Congress and signed into public law in late 2008. Although this act focuses heavily on providing improved broadband access to various locations in the United States, some sections of the act, such as section 215, address creating a safe Internet for children. The act requires schools with Internet access to educate students about appropriate online behavior, which includes interacting with others in chat rooms and on social networking sites. Additionally, the act requires that students are to be educated to recognize and appropriately respond to cyberbullying. The full language of this act is available online at www.govtrack.us/congress/billtext.xpd?bill=s110–1492.

To provide guidelines for using technology at school, school districts develop an acceptable use policy (AUP). An AUP outlines rules and responsibilities for students who use district- and school-purchased technology. Additionally, an AUP includes the consequences for failing to follow the rules. AUPs usually identify when and how students can utilize district-purchased computers and Internet connections, the nature of the content that can be viewed or downloaded, and descriptions of content that are unacceptable to access. Generally, all students and their parents are expected to sign the agreement before students are allowed to access the Internet at school. Most school districts also create a separate AUP that outlines what is considered acceptable use for teachers and school employees. In broad terms, most AUPs state that digital technologies of any kind may only be used for sanctioned classwork and school activities.

Predators, or Ensnaring Young People

The first step in reporting a crime of child exploitation, according to the U.S. Department of Justice, is to contact a local FBI office. The FBI maintains 56 field offices in major metropolitan areas throughout the United States and Puerto Rico. The FBI maintains an interactive website (www.fbi.gov/contact/fo/fo.htm) that makes locating and contacting its local offices relatively easy. There is also a toll-free number for calling in reports: 1.800.CALLFBI (225.5324).

Another resource for reporting a child exploitation crime is the National Center for Missing and Exploited Children (NCMEC), which operates a website where parents and children can report child pornography and other incidents of sexual exploitation by filling out and submitting an online form. The NCMEC also maintains a 24-hour hotline: 1.800.THE.LOST (843.5678) and a website with current information on missing and exploited children (www.missingkids.com).

Misuse of Mobile Communication Devices and Cyberbullying

Freedom of speech and defamation of character are the major legal issues associated with recording and texting in the classroom. There are several cases in which students have been suspended from school because they recorded teachers and fellow students and then posted this information on a personal web page or on a social network site, such as Facebook or MySpace. The suspensions have been challenged on the grounds that students have the right to the freedom of speech. The rulings on these cases vary. What is important to note is that there does not seem to be a clear consensus regarding the recording of what takes places in schools. Many schools have taken the stance of banning these devices on the grounds that they are disruptive to the school environment because they interfere with teaching and learning. In more than one case, parents have legally challenged the ban of these devices—primarily the ban of cell phones—stating that they, as parents, have the right to be able to contact their children at any time, especially if there is an emergency or a school crisis.

Additionally, administrators and teachers should be aware of the laws and policies that exist regarding cyberbullying. These are often tied to current anti-bullying laws and policies. Although there is not a national law against cyberbullying, as of early 2009, more than a dozen states had passed laws and policies on cyberbullying. Administrators should examine these laws and policies and pass along their key elements to teachers and parents.

Inappropriate Uses of the Network

Inappropriate uses of school networks are typically outlined in an AUP. An AUP describes guidelines for how staff and students may use a school network and the consequences for not following the guidelines. In general, the various laws and regulations associated with the other technology threats described in this book bind an individual's use of a school's network.

Copyright Infringement

Copyright infringement is one of the most misunderstood threats that schools face. Although not a threat that will bring personal harm to staff and students, copyright infringement is still a serious issue that administrators and teachers need to understand. Teachers can violate copyright law unknowingly. The major issues administrators and students should understand regarding copyright are fair use and the Technology, Education and Copyright Harmonization (TEACH) Act.

The U.S. Copyright Office states that exclusive rights to intellectual property have limitations, and "… use by reproduction in copies or phonorecords or by any other means specified by that section, for purposes such as criticism, comment, news reporting, teaching (including multiple copies for classroom use), scholarship, or research, is not an infringement of copyright, …" (U.S. Copyright Office, 2009a).

In determining whether fair use is made of a work in any particular case, a judge considers the following factors:

- Whether use is of a commercial nature or is for nonprofit educational purposes

- The nature of the copyrighted work itself

- The amount used and the importance of that amount in relation to the copyrighted work as a whole

- The effect of the use upon the potential market for or value of the work. (U.S. Copyright Office, 2009a)

The fair use doctrine is a set of guidelines used by court judges to determine whether copyright infringement has occurred. It is important to keep in mind that these are guidelines and not a specific formula; only a court judge may determine whether copyright infringement has occurred or if the work is being used fairly, and that happens only if a suit is brought by the copyright owner.

The TEACH Act, signed by President Bush in 2002, is an attempt to provide clarification and greater latitude for use of copyrighted materials by educators in networked computing settings. The TEACH Act allows educators working in accredited nonprofit educational settings to make use of copyrighted materials for the purpose of instruction. The use of copyrighted materials must be limited to the number of students enrolled in a specific class and does not include rights to distribute textbook materials or other materials students would typically purchase. It also does not allow use of copyrighted materials for which the owners have expressly forbidden copy or redistribution (Copyright Clearance Center, 2005).

Data and Identity Theft

The Family Educational Rights and Privacy Act (FERPA), the Protection of Pupil Rights Amendment (PPRA), the National School Lunch Act (NSLA), and the Individuals with Disabilities Education Act (IDEA) are major examples of federal laws that dictate how student data is to be treated. In examining various states' laws, we found that California, for example, has passed several laws that impact the treatment of student data. California Education Code 60641 and the Individual Privacy Act (IPA) California Civil Code 1798.24 are two such laws (California Legislative Analyst's Office, 2008). Data theft can place schools in violation of these laws. Administrators, in particular, could be held primarily responsible for data theft that occurs through any means—such as the loss of a school-owned laptop or individuals hacking into the school network. It is important for administrators to read through these laws and regulations.

Parting Advice

British philosopher Francis Bacon wrote that knowledge is power (1597). When it comes to technology use in schools, this statement rings true for administrators and teachers. The more knowledge administrators, teachers, parents, and information technology specialists have about the threats of technology use in schools, the better able they will be to make decisions regarding how to use technology effectively. Coupled with this knowledge, everyone should be aware of the rules and regulations associated with technology. This requires continual professional development, beginning with exploring some of the numerous sources available on the web. The National School Board Association's (NSBA) website (www.nsba.org) is a practical starting point. On the NSBA website, search for the school law link that provides access to a web page that discusses federal regulations and court case summaries impacting schools.

References

Anderson, M. (2006). *Identity Theft and Middle School Students*. Retrieved on November 13, 2008, from www.identitytheftfixes.com/identity_theft_and_middle_school_students.html

Awdeh, D. M., & Esquenet, M. A. (2007, December). Linking rights to sites. *Copyright World*. Retrieved November 18, 2009, from www.finnegan.com/resources/articles/articlesdetail.aspx?news=9f94f135-b29b-4f62-8226-8c0e3ac0892a

Bacon, Francis. (1597). Religious Meditations, Of Heresies.

Baig, E. C. (2003, January 29). Keeping Internet predators at bay. *USA Today*. Retrieved from www.usatoday.com/tech/columnist/edwardbaig/2003-01-29-baig-safety_x.htm

Becker, H. J. (2000). Findings from the teaching, learning, and computing survey: Is Larry Cuban right? *Education Policy Analysis Archives, 8*(51). Available from http://epaa.asu.edu/epaa/v8n51

Berkeley schools restore Internet. (2008, April 29). *The Post and Courier*. Retrieved from www.postandcourier.com/news/2008/apr/29/berkeley_schools_restore_internet38968

Broadband Data Improvement Act, Pub. L. No. 110-385 (2008). Senate bill version S. 1492. www.govtrack.us/congress/billtext.xpd?bill=s110-1492

California Education Code 60641. (2008). Sacramento, CA: Legislative Analyst's Office.

California Individual Privacy Act (IPA). California Civil Code 1798.24. (2008). Sacramento, CA: Legislative Analyst's Office. Retrieved on November 13, 2008, from www.lao.ca.gov/2008/edu/student_data_access/student_data_access.aspx

Carter, D. (2008, July 15). Getting a grasp on student hackers. *eSchool News*. Retrieved from www.eschoolnews.com/resources/keeping-online-learning-secure/keeping-online-learning-secure-articles/index.cfm?rc=1&i=54540

Carvin, A. (2008). *Questioning the notion of online predators.* Retrieved September 10, 2008, from www.pbs.org/teachers/learning.now/2008/02/questioning_the_notion_of_onli.html

CEO Forum on Education and Technology. (1999). *The CEO Forum school technology and readiness, Report 2: Professional development, a link to better learning.* Washington, DC: Author.

Cheung, H. (2008, June 18). High school student faces 38 years in prison for hacking grades. *Business and Law.* Retrieved November 18, 2009, from www.tgdaily.com/content/view/38012/118/tgdaily

Children's Internet Protection Act (CIPA). (2001). Federal Communications Commission, Consumer and Governmental Affairs Bureau. Retrieved from www.fcc.gov/cgb/consumerfacts/cipa.html

Copyright Clearance Center. (2005). *The TEACH Act: New rules, roles, and responsibilities for academic institutions.* Danvers, MA: Author. Retrieved September 29, 2008, from www.copyright.com/media/pdfs/CR-Teach-Act.pdf

Crook, C., Fisher, T., Graber, R., Harrison, C., Lewin, C., Cummings, J., Logan, K., Luckin, R., Oliver, M., & Sharples, M. (2008). *Implementing web 2.0 in secondary schools: Impacts, barriers and issues.* Coventry, UK: Becta. Available from www.becta.org.uk

Cuban, L., Kirkpatrick, H., & Peck, C. (2001). High access and low use of technologies in high school classrooms: Explaining an apparent paradox. *American Educational Research Journal, 38*(4), 813–834.

Davis, V. (2007). *Wikis in the classroom.* Retrieved October 1, 2008, from www.slideshare.net/coolcatteacher/wikis-in-the-classroom

Devaney, L. (2007, July 13). Education the key to better security. *eSchool News.* Retrieved from www.eschoolnews.com/resources/safeguarding-school-data/safeguarding-school-data-articles/index.cfm?rc=1&i=46444

District posts confidential data online: Unsecured servers expose information for some 7,500 Indianapolis students. (2007, May 21). *eSchool News.* Retrieved from www.eschoolnews.com/resources/safeguarding-school-data/safeguarding-school-data-articles/index.cfm?rc=1&i=46185

Dodds, R., & Mason, C. Y. (2005). Cell phones and pda's hit K–6. *Education Digest. 70*(8), 52–53.

Ebbeling, V. (2008, August 31). Students find new ways to cheat from texting to Internet: Students employ new ways to break the rules on papers and tests. *Press & Sun-Bulletin.* Available from www.pressconnects.com

Ertmer, P. A., Addison, P., Lane, M., Ross, E., & Woods, D. (1999). Examining teachers' beliefs about the role of technology in the elementary classroom. *Journal of Research on Computing in Education, 32*(1), 54–62.

Etter, L. (2004, September 17). Technology (a special report); putting tech to the test: As students turn to high-tech gadgets to cheat, schools consider turning to high-tech gadgets to stop them. *The Wall Street Journal,* p. R17.

Family Educational Rights and Privacy Act (FERPA). Retrieved from www.ed.gov/policy/gen/guid/fpco/ferpa/index.html

Federal Bureau of Investigation. (n.d.*a*). Innocent Images National Initiative. Retrieved from www.fbi.gov/innocent.htm

Federal Bureau of Investigation. (n.d.*b*). Safety tips: Internet safety. Retrieved from www.fbi.gov/kids/k5th/safety2.htm

Finkelhor, D. (Speaker). (2008, January 22). *Frontline: The predator fear.* [Television broadcast and transcription]. Boston: WGBH Educational Foundation. Retrieved September 6, 2008, from www.pbs.org/wgbh/pages/frontline/kidsonline/safe/predator.html#finkelhor

Fryer, W. A. (2003, August 28). A beginner's guide to school security. *Technology & Learning.* Retrieved from www.techlearning.com/article/13824

Gillespie, I. (2008, April 16). Teaching students to navigate digital diversions. *London Free Press.* Available from www.lfpress.com

Harmon, A. (2006, August 26). Internet gives teenage bullies weapons to wound from afar. *The New York Times.* Retrieved from www.nytimes.com/2004/08/26/education/26bully.html?ex=1251172800&en=75fc821f51c20daf&ei=5088&partner=rssnyt

Heins, M., Cho, C., & Feldman, A. (2006). *Internet filters: A public policy report.* Brennan Center for Justice, New York School of Law. Retrieved March 20, 2009, from www.fepproject.org/policyreports/filters2.pdf

High school limits student cell phone use. (2002, January 21). *Associated Press.* Retrieved from www.usatoday.com/tech/news/2002/01/21/schools-cell-phones.htm

Hinduja, S., & Patchin, J. W. (2005). *Research summary: Cyberbullying victimization. Preliminary findings from an online survey of Internet-using adolescents.* Retrieved from www.cyberbullying.us/cyberbullying_victimization.pdf

Hinduja, S., & Patchin, J. W. (2008). Cyberbullying: An exploratory analysis of factors related to offending and victimization. *Deviant Behavior, 29*(2), 129–156.

Hitlin, P., & Rainie, L. (2005). *Data memo: Teens, technology, and school.* Pew Internet & American Life Project. Available from www.pewinternet.org

HK teens build 'terror' bomb: Police. (2009, March 29). *Agence France-Presse*. Retrieved from http://news.theage.com.au/breaking-news-world/hk-teens-build-terror-bomb-police-20090329-9fg4.html

Hobbs, R. (2008, March 12). Copyright confusion is shortchanging our students. *Education Week*. Retrieved from www.edweek.org/ew/articles/2008/03/12/27hobbs.h27.html?qs=copyright+confusion

Hobbs, R., Jaszi, P., & Aufderheide, P. (2007). *The cost of copyright confusion for media literacy*. Washington, DC: Center for Social Media.

International Society for Technology in Education (ISTE). (2000). *National educational technology standards for teachers* (1st ed.). Eugene, OR: Author. Also available online at www.iste.org/Content/NavigationMenu/NETS/ForTeachers/2000Standards/NETS_for_Teachers_2000.htm

International Society for Technology in Education (ISTE). (2008). *National educational technology standards for teachers* (2nd ed.). Eugene, OR: Author. Also available online at www.iste.org/Content/NavigationMenu/NETS/ForTeachers/2008Standards/NETS_for_Teachers_2008.htm

i-Safe. (2004). *National i-Safe survey*. Carlsbad, CA: Author.

Johnson, L., & Lamb, A. (2007). *Teacher tap: Copyright issues*. Retrieved September 27, 2008, from http://eduscapes.com/tap/topic24.htm

Kaiser Family Foundation. (2005). *Generation M: Media in the lives of 8–18 year-olds*. Menlo Park, CA: Author.

Kalkowski, M. A. (2001). Focus on learning and technology. *Communication: Journalism Education Today, 34*(4), 19–22, 25, 27.

Kamaron Institute. (2008). Cyber bullying solutions. Available from http://kamaron.org/Cyber-Bullying-Solutions

Kolb, L. (2008). *Toys to tools: Connecting student cell phones to education*. Eugene, OR: International Society for Technology in Education (ISTE).

Kowalski, R., & Limber, S. (2007). Electronic bullying among middle school students. *Journal of Adolescent Health, 42,* S22–S30.

Laptop theft puts 40,000 school employees at risk. (2007, May 17). *eSchool News.* Retrieved December 18, 2009 from www.eschoolnews. com/resources/safeguarding-school-data/safeguarding-school-data-articles/index.cfm?rc=1&i=46155

Livingstone, S., & Bober, M. (2005). *UK children go online: Final report of key project findings.* London: Media@LSE. Available from www.citizensonline.org.uk/publications

Macgill, Alexandra R. (2007). *Data memo: Parent and teenager Internet use.* Pew Internet & American Life Project. Available from www.pewinternet.org

Maull, S. (2007, May 7). State court says city can ban cell phone. *New York Daily News.* Retrieved from www.nydailynews.com/news/2007/05/07/2007-05-07_state_court_says_city_can_ban_cell_phone.html

McCord Hoffman, G. (2001). *Copyright in cyberspace.* New York: Neal-Schuman Publishers, Inc.

Menillo, M. (2009, April 1). Off the streets … and online. *NetSmartz Workshop.* National Center for Missing and Exploited Children. Retrieved December 24, 2009, from http://uyn.blogspot.com/2009/04/gangs-off-streetsand-online_1437.html

Murray, C. (2004, June 22). Copyright excesses worry teachers, scholars. *eSchool News.* Retrieved from www.eschoolnews.com/news/top-news/index.cfm?i=35823&CFID=23294478&CFTOKEN=36457761

National Center for Missing and Exploited Children. (2008). *Online enticement of children for sexual acts.* Retrieved December 11, 2009, from www.missingkids.com/missingkids/servlet/PageServlet?LanguageCountry=en_US&PageId=1503

National Crime Prevention Council. (2007, October 1). Delete cyberbullying. *2007 Celebrate Crime Prevention Newspaper Supplement.* Available from www.ncpc.org/programs/crime-prevention-month/newspaper-supplements

National survey shows parents' fear of sexual predators and abductors on school campuses. (2008, August 19). *Business Wire.* Retrieved May 9, 2009, from www.allbusiness.com/society social/families-children-family-members/11489400-1.html

NOLO. (2008). *The 'fair use' rule: When use of copyrighted material is acceptable.* NOLOPEDIA: Patents, Copyright & Art. Retrieved from www.nolo.com/legal-encyclopedia/article-30100.com

Patchin, J., & Hinduja, S. (2006). Bullies move beyond the schoolyard: A preliminary look at cyberbullying. *Youth Violence and Juvenile Justice, 4*(2), 148–169.

Prensky, M. (2005). What can you learn from a cell phone? Almost anything! *Innovate Journal of Online Education, 1*(5). Available from www.innovateonline.info

Project Tomorrow. (2008). *Speak up 2007 for students, teachers, parents and school leaders: Selected National Findings, April 8, 2008.* Available from www.tomorrow.org

Protection of Pupil Rights Amendment (PPRA). Retrieved from www.ed.gov/policy/gen/guid/fpco/ppra/index.html

RIAA cracks down on downloading at 25 colleges. (2007, February 21). *ZDNet.* Retrieved September 29, 2008, from http://education.zdnet.com/?p=862

Robinson, L. (2003). *Diffusion of educational technology and education reform: A qualitative study of educators' perceived barriers.* Unpublished doctoral dissertation, Washington State University, Pullman.

Robinson, L., Brown, A., & Green, T. (2004, October). *The threat of security: Increased technology access limitations on teachers and students.* Paper presented at the Association of Educational Communications and Technology Annual Conference, Chicago, IL.

Robinson, L., Brown, A., & Green, T. (2007). Hindering technology integration in the classroom: The threat of security. *Learning & Leading with Technology, 35*(2), 19–23.

S. 49—110th Congress: Protecting Children in the 21st Century Act. (2007). In *GovTrack.us (database of federal legislation).* Retrieved June 25, 2008, from www.govtrack.us/congress/bill.xpd?bill=s110-49

Sandoval, G. (2008, July 22). Viacom CEO Philippe Dauman on Google's 'rogue company.' *CNET News.* Available from http://news.cnet.com/8301-1023_3-9996383-93.html?tag=mncol;txt

Schools ban iPods to prevent cheating. (2007, April 30). *Associated Press.* Retrieved December 17, 2009, from www.foxnews.com/story/0,2933,268903,00.html

Schwartz, K. D. (2008, August/September). Stop, thief! Software helps schools track lost or stolen notebooks. *EdTech* K–12. Retrieved on November 13, 2008, from www.edtechmag.com/k12/issues/august-september-2008/stop-thief.html

Set up a velvet rope on Facebook. (2008). Retrieved September 6, 2008, from Wired How-To Wiki: http://howto.wired.com/wiki/Set_Up_a_Velvet_Rope_on_Facebook

Shukovsky, P., & Akhmeteli, N. (2007, May 22). Free speech vs. class disruption: Court to decide if teen can be suspended over video of teacher. *Seatle Post Intelligencer.* Available from http://seattlepi.nwsource.com/local/316618_youtube22.html

Stone, B. (2007, May 15). States fault MySpace on predator issues. *The New York Times.* Available from www.nytimes.com/2007/05/15/technology/15myspace.html?_r=1

Surdin, A. (2009, January 1). In several states, a push to stem cyber-bullying: Most of the laws focus on schools. *The Washington Post.* Available from www.washingtonpost.com/wp-dyn/content/article/2008/12/31/AR2008123103067.html

Technology, Education and Copyright Harmonization (TEACH) Act (subtitle C of title III of H. R. 2215, originally S. 487). (2002). Available from the Library of Congress: www.loc.gov/index.html

Templeton, B. (2008). 10 big myths about copyright explained. Retrieved December 17, 2009, from www.templetons.com/brad/copymyths.html

U.S. Copyright Office. (2006). *Copyright in general.* Retrieved December 17, 2009, from www.copyright.gov/help/faq/faq-general.html#what

U.S. Copyright Office. (2008). *Copyright Basics* (Circular 1). Washington, DC: Library of Congress. Available from www.copyright.gov

U.S. Copyright Office. (2009a). *Reproduction of copyrighted works by educators and librarians* (Circular 21). Washington, DC: Library of Congress. Available from www.copyright.gov

U.S. Copyright Office. (2009b). *Can I use someone else's work? Can someone else use mine?* Retrieved December 17, 2009, from www.copyright.gov/help/faq/faq-fairuse.html#permission

U.S. Department of Justice. (2006). *Cyberethics for teachers: A lesson plan outline for elementary and middle school children.* Retrieved September 6, 2008, from www.usdoj.gov/criminal/cybercrime/rules/lessonplan1.htm

Williams, P. (2006, February 3). MySpace, Facebook attract online predators: Experts say be careful what you post online—somebody is always watching. *NBC News.* Retrieved September 10, 2008, from www.msnbc.msn.com/id/11165576

With PC tracking software, stolen laptop recovered almost instantly. *eSchool News.* (2002, July 1). Retrieved December 18, 2009 from www.eschoolnews.com/resources/safeguarding-school-data/safeguarding-school-data-articles/index.cfm?rc=1&i=34583

Wolak, J., Finkelhor, D., Mitchell, K. J., and Ybarra, M. L. (2008). Online "predators" and their victims: Myths, realities, and implications for prevention and treatment. *American Psychologist, 63*(2), 111–128.

Wolak, J., Mitchell, K., & Finkelhor, D. (2006). *Online victimization of youth: Five years later.* Alexandria, VA: National Center for Missing and Exploited Children.

Workman, L. (2007). *Does your family know how to be safe on the Internet?* Retrieved April 7, 2009, from www.ikeepsafe.org/iksc_about/news/?action=display_article&article_id=113

Yang, G., Wong, D. S., Huang, Q., & Deng, X. (2007). A new security definition for public key encryption schemes and its applications. *Cryptology ePrint Archive.* Retrieved on December 24, 2009 from http://eprint.iacr.org/2007/319.pdf

Zeltser, L. (2008, October 1). Security: Where the risks are. *Campus Technology.* Retrieved October 8, 2008, http://campustechnology.com/articles/68095

Additional Readings and Resources

Bailey, G., & Ribble, M. (2007). *Digital citizenship in schools.* Eugene, OR: International Society for Technology in Education (ISTE).

Campbell, S. (2006). Perceptions of mobile phones in college classrooms: Ringing, cheating, and classroom policies. *Communication Education, 55*(3), 280–294.

Elgin, M. (2007, May 4). Are iPod-banning schools cheating our kids? Why iPods and other electronic gadgets should be required, not banned. *Computerworld.* www.computerworld.com/action/article.do?command=viewArticleBasic&articleId=9018594

Federal Bureau of Investigation. (n.d.) Your local FBI office. Interactive website: www.fbi.gov/contact/fo/fo.htm. Toll-free number for calling in reports: 1.800.CALLFBI (225.5324).

Gerard, V. (2006). Updating policy on latest risks for students with cell phones in the school. *Education Digest, 72*(4), 43–45.

Guhlin, M. (2006, August 1). Encrypt your data to avoid identity theft. *Technology & Learning.* Retrieved on November 13, 2008, from www.techlearning.com/story/showArticle.php?articleID=190301930

Individuals with Disabilities Education Act (IDEA). Website: http://idea.ed.gov

International Society for Technology in Education (ISTE). (2009). *National educational technology standards for administrators* (2nd ed.). Eugene, OR: Author. Also available online at www.iste.org/Content/NavigationMenu/NETS/ForAdministrators/2009Standards/NETS_for_Administrators_2009.htm

Mallory, A. L. (2008, January 20). Fending off digital thieves: Guarding Virginia Tech's vast computer network and users' privacy is a full-time job. *The Roanoke Times.* Retrieved December 18, 2009, from www.roanoke.com/news/nrv/wb/147727

National Center for Missing and Exploited Children (NCMEC). Website: www.cybertipline.com. The NCMEC's 24-hour hotline: 1.800.THE.LOST (843.5678) and website: www.missingkids.com

National School Boards Association. Website: www.nsba.org

Walker, M. (2004, September 10). High-tech cribbing: Camera phones facilitate cheating. *The Wall Street Journal,* p. B1.

National Educational Technology Standards

National Educational Technology Standards for Teachers (NETS•T)

All classroom teachers should be prepared to meet the following standards and performance indicators. Teachers:

1. Facilitate and Inspire Student Learning and Creativity

Teachers use their knowledge of subject matter, teaching and learning, and technology to facilitate experiences that advance student learning, creativity, and innovation in both face-to-face and virtual environments. Teachers:

a. promote, support, and model creative and innovative thinking and inventiveness

b. engage students in exploring real-world issues and solving authentic problems using digital tools and resources

c. promote student reflection using collaborative tools to reveal and clarify students' conceptual understanding and thinking, planning, and creative processes

d. model collaborative knowledge construction by engaging in learning with students, colleagues, and others in face-to-face and virtual environments

2. Design and Develop Digital-Age Learning Experiences and Assessments

Teachers design, develop, and evaluate authentic learning experiences and assessments incorporating contemporary tools and resources to maximize content learning in context and to develop the knowledge, skills, and attitudes identified in the NETS•S. Teachers:

    a. design or adapt relevant learning experiences that incorporate digital tools and resources to promote student learning and creativity

    b. develop technology-enriched learning environments that enable all students to pursue their individual curiosities and become active participants in setting their own educational goals, managing their own learning, and assessing their own progress

    c. customize and personalize learning activities to address students' diverse learning styles, working strategies, and abilities using digital tools and resources

    d. provide students with multiple and varied formative and summative assessments aligned with content and technology standards and use resulting data to inform learning and teaching

3. Model Digital-Age Work and Learning

Teachers exhibit knowledge, skills, and work processes representative of an innovative professional in a global and digital society. Teachers:

    a. demonstrate fluency in technology systems and the transfer of current knowledge to new technologies and situations

    b. collaborate with students, peers, parents, and community members using digital tools and resources to support student success and innovation

    c. communicate relevant information and ideas effectively to students, parents, and peers using a variety of digital-age media and formats

    d. model and facilitate effective use of current and emerging digital tools to locate, analyze, evaluate, and use information resources to support research and learning

4. Promote and Model Digital Citizenship and Responsibility

Teachers understand local and global societal issues and responsibilities in an evolving digital culture and exhibit legal and ethical behavior in their professional practices. Teachers:

    a. advocate, model, and teach safe, legal, and ethical use of digital information and technology, including respect for copyright, intellectual property, and the appropriate documentation of sources

    b. address the diverse needs of all learners by using learner-centered strategies and providing equitable access to appropriate digital tools and resources

    c. promote and model digital etiquette and responsible social interactions related to the use of technology and information

    d. develop and model cultural understanding and global awareness by engaging with colleagues and students of other cultures using digital-age communication and collaboration tools

5. Engage in Professional Growth and Leadership

Teachers continuously improve their professional practice, model lifelong learning, and exhibit leadership in their school and professional community by promoting and demonstrating the effective use of digital tools and resources. Teachers:

    a. participate in local and global learning communities to explore creative applications of technology to improve student learning

    b. exhibit leadership by demonstrating a vision of technology infusion, participating in shared decision making and community building, and developing the leadership and technology skills of others

    c. evaluate and reflect on current research and professional practice on a regular basis to make effective use of existing and emerging digital tools and resources in support of student learning

    d. contribute to the effectiveness, vitality, and self-renewal of the teaching profession and of their school and community

National Educational Technology Standards for Administrators (NETS•A)

All school administrators should be prepared to meet the following standards and performance indicators.

1. Visionary Leadership

Educational Administrators inspire and lead development and implementation of a shared vision for comprehensive integration of technology to promote excellence and support transformation throughout the organization. Educational Administrators:

   a. inspire and facilitate among all stakeholders a shared vision of purposeful change that maximizes use of digital-age resources to meet and exceed learning goals, support effective instructional practice, and maximize performance of district and school leaders

   b. engage in an ongoing process to develop, implement, and communicate technology-infused strategic plans aligned with a shared vision

   c. advocate on local, state, and national levels for policies, programs, and funding to support implementation of a technology-infused vision and strategic plan

2. Digital-Age Learning Culture

Educational Administrators create, promote, and sustain a dynamic, digital-age learning culture that provides a rigorous, relevant, and engaging education for all students. Educational Administrators:

   a. ensure instructional innovation focused on continuous improvement of digital-age learning

    b. model and promote the frequent and effective use of technology for learning

    c. provide learner-centered environments equipped with technology and learning resources to meet the individual, diverse needs of all learners

    d. ensure effective practice in the study of technology and its infusion across the curriculum

    e. promote and participate in local, national, and global learning communities that stimulate innovation, creativity, and digital-age collaboration

3. Excellence in Professional Practice

Educational Administrators promote an environment of professional learning and innovation that empowers educators to enhance student learning through the infusion of contemporary technologies and digital resources. Educational Administrators:

    a. allocate time, resources, and access to ensure ongoing professional growth in technology fluency and integration

    b. facilitate and participate in learning communities that stimulate, nurture, and support administrators, faculty, and staff in the study and use of technology

    c. promote and model effective communication and collaboration among stakeholders using digital-age tools

    d. stay abreast of educational research and emerging trends regarding effective use of technology and encourage evaluation of new technologies for their potential to improve student learning

4. Systemic Improvement

Educational Administrators provide digital-age leadership and management to continuously improve the organization through the effective use of information and technology resources. Educational Administrators:

    a. lead purposeful change to maximize the achievement of learning goals through the appropriate use of technology and media-rich resources

    b. collaborate to establish metrics, collect and analyze data, interpret results, and share findings to improve staff performance and student learning

    c. recruit and retain highly competent personnel who use technology creatively and proficiently to advance academic and operational goals

    d. establish and leverage strategic partnerships to support systemic improvement

    e. establish and maintain a robust infrastructure for technology including integrated, interoperable technology systems to support management, operations, teaching, and learning

5. Digital Citizenship

Educational Administrators model and facilitate understanding of social, ethical, and legal issues and responsibilities related to an evolving digital culture. Educational Administrators:

    a. ensure equitable access to appropriate digital tools and resources to meet the needs of all learners

    b. promote, model, and establish policies for safe, legal, and ethical use of digital information and technology

   c. promote and model responsible social interactions related to the use of technology and information

   d. model and facilitate the development of a shared cultural understanding and involvement in global issues through the use of contemporary communication and collaboration tools